Cover design
Skip Moen

THE HIDDEN BEAST

Confronting the Enemy Within

Skip Moen

Tikkun 'olam is the Jewish idea of the restoration of the world. While it is usually focused on social and political environments, there is a sense in which *tikkun 'olam* cannot begin in the outside world until it has taken root in the *inside* world. We need personal *tikkun 'olam*, personal restoration. We need to begin by restoring what God intended for each of us. To do that, we will have to confront the enemy of *tikkun 'olam*, **the beast within** each of us, the *yetzer ha'ra*, that force of ego that wants the world its way. The most virulent form of the *yetzer ha'ra* is addiction because addiction is the *personal* neuro-physical mismanagement of life's trauma and emotions. Trauma and emotions are inevitable. How we manage them is not. That is the purpose of understanding and applying what we learn here.

Skip Moen
Montverde
February 2017

And do not be conformed to this world, but be transformed by the renewing of your mind that you may prove what the will of God is, that which is good and acceptable and perfect. Romans 12:2

We are destroying speculations and every lofty thing raised up against the knowledge of God, and we are taking every thought captive to the obedience of Christ. 2 Corinthians 10:5

So then do not be foolish, but understand what the will of the Lord is. Ephesians 5:17

"Since the inner world is sacred, the outer world must be kept clean."
Abraham Joshua Heschel

Acknowledgements

Many people have been part of this book. Some helped me in the distant past and are no longer in the fight. Jerry was one of them. Some are recent contributors. Among them are Cyndee and Donna who took the time to look over the manuscript and make corrections. Zelda offered counsel that helped me formulate the idea itself. But the one who really matters here is Rosanne who has lived with the man in the fight for a long time. She is a warrior woman.

Thank you, all.

Table of Contents

INTRODUCTION

I'm Sick

I just want to throw up! Just put my head in the toilet of the universe and vomit out all my ailments – the hurts, the disappointments, failures, jealousy and envy, anger and depression, lies, cheating, manipulations. I want to clean me out. I feel like a New York street during a summer garbage strike. Something stinks inside. But as much as I want to throw it all up, I can't. I just can't gag myself into getting rid of *me*.

I am learning not to pretend. It's my key to correct prognosis. Facing who I really am means that I have to stop fooling myself. It's not easy. I have years and years of cover-up messages to rewind. There are times when I know that I can never *think* my way to understanding what's good for me. I have programmed myself with so many "excuse" tapes that my very thinking is unreliable. How do I know that I can't trust my own thoughts? Because saying "I'm fine" is a lie, even to me. I'm not fine. I hurt! and I just can't fool myself anymore.

Something isn't quite right. I can't put my finger on it, but I know that there is this permanent need for Tums for what I do – enough to remind me that all my systems are not quite synchronized with each other. I get depressed when I think about it. I'd like to pull up the covers and go back to sleep. Maybe things would look different if I got out on the other side of bed. In my heart, I know that they won't. The sickness isn't on the outside. It's in me, somewhere, doing damage.

I'm afraid to face it. Like people who suspect they have terminal cancer but refuse to go in for tests. As if ignoring and pretending will somehow make it go away. Modern medicine man magic. But it doesn't work. The sickness is progressive. I can force myself to go on, there are plenty of distractions available, but it never goes away. And it grows. Malignant.

When my mind functions on those occasions when the nausea is in recession, I know that I need radical surgery. But I don't know where to go to get it. I don't know who has the right skills with the knife. And I don't want to bleed. I'm afraid that if someone were to cut out this tumor, the bleeding would never stop. Or maybe they would find that the disease had spread through all of me. Either way, I'm afraid to die. Just like the old blues song, "Everybody wants to go to heaven, but nobody wants to die."

I tell myself that it is better to live now even if living is just slow death. But I know it's a lie. Death is death. Fast or slow, it steals my joy of being. It corrupts my hopes. It poisons my loves. Death isn't life no matter how often I lie to myself. If I want to live, to fill my lungs with the air of inner peace, I will have to cut. I will have to bleed. I will have to leave parts of me on the surgeon's table. For me to live, something will have to die.

"The strength of holiness lies underground, in the somatic. It is primarily in the way in which we gratify physical needs that the seed of holiness is planted . . . involved, immersed in common and earthly endeavors; carried primarily by individual, private, simple deeds rather than public ceremonies."[1]

---

[1] Abraham Heschel, *Between God and Man: An Interpretation of Judaism* (Free Press, New York, 1959) p. 147.

PART ONE

CHAPTER ONE

Body Consciousness

Self-examination has become essential for modern
life. Women are encouraged to feel for unusual
lumps in the breast. Men are challenged to stop
ignoring digestive upsets. We are all asked to pay
attention to our bodies, to understand that they are
not machines, to be aware of the signals they send
us about their condition. Our generation has been
sensitized to the threats of cancer, stress, heart
disease and other maladies through routine self-
exams. But for some reason, we have given much
less attention to a critical area requiring intensive
self-examination. In fact, not only is this area of
our lives far more important than any of the body
functions we try to monitor, it can *only* be accessed
by self-examination. There are no EKGs, no X-
rays, no mammograms or CAT scans to determine
the progress of the disease, but it is a killer
nevertheless. Furthermore, it is perfectly capable of
destroying every part of our carefully attended
physical systems as well as our mental and
emotional sense of well-being.

Given these facts, no higher priority could exist
than the rigorous self-examination needed to
uncover this killer. Logic would certainly suggest
that we should spend whatever effort and time

necessary to eradicate this threat to our very existence. Nevertheless, we seem quite complacent about our frightful situation. We regard this killer on the same level as gum disease. Of course, we know that it is there, slowly and inevitably destroying the foundation of our teeth, but it doesn't hurt now and it doesn't seem to make a lot of difference to the way that we want to live, so it is ignored. Like gum disease, we tell ourselves we can manage without paying attention to it. But unlike gum disease, this malady is absolutely fatal. It will kill us if it hasn't already done so, whether we make ourselves aware of its effect or not.

There are a great many reasons given for blissful deliberate ignorance. They are as common as they are insipid. The first is that the disease itself is a fiction, invented by those who would claim to be able to treat it. The second is that if I feel no immediate discomfort, I must not have the disease. The third is that I am not in excruciating pain, so the disease, even if it exists, cannot be acute. The fourth is that even if I do have the disease, there seems to be nothing that I can do about it. The fifth is that I recognize that I am sick, but it's not possible to control the spread of the disease, so why bother?

What kind of sickness is it that would elicit all of these responses? What kind of illness can *only* be discovered by the patient and is resistant to any form of outside human intervention? It is the soul sickness—the cancer of emotionally dysfunctional sins.

Diagnosis

If I am concerned enough to start the self-examination of my emotional mismanagement, the surgery starts with a sliver of graphite on a piece of wood pulp. Pencil and paper. I can't get well if I don't know what's wrong. And I can't know what's wrong if I deny the dissonance between my thoughts and my actions. Already I encounter my first enemy – denial. I hear the messages. "I'm not so bad." "I'm better than she is." "It just depends on your point-of-view." "Everyone has his faults." "That isn't really me." They go on and on. I have thousands of them. I have been practicing them, improving them, adapting them all my life. How can clean water come from a polluted spring? If I look carefully at my actions, I know there is something wrong. The excuses only provide camouflage. In the end, I know I am not as good as I pretend to be. I realize that I can't trust myself. If I am to truly understand my condition, I'll need a sharper instrument than my own reason to penetrate this callused skin. Even as I write this line, I am already aware that I want to find a way to escape the coming evaluation.

I am what I do. There is truth in that. My behaviors don't lie about me. They don't say anything at all. They just gush forth. "But the water looks good to others?" That's my justification trying to find a way to reconcile the conflicts. But the actions stand. I can't deny my cheating. I can't ignore my fighting. I can't dispute my lying. I can't falsify my anger. I did it. It was me (even if I felt like an alien). I own it.

Pick up the pencil. One word descriptions. One word memos that say who I really see in the mirror. One word that says who I feel I am, right now. One word without excuses, pretenses or denial. To get there, I will have to write down how I behave. My life in screenplay script. Behaviors I would rather forget. Behaviors I have refused to believe. All those things that weren't me. The Bible calls them "sins of the flesh."

The time that I deliberately tried to injure my brother. The time I pushed my best friend down a ladder to save myself. The time I ran away. The time I stole something at the store. The time I lied. The time I used someone else to satisfy my impulse. I time I made up a story. I time I took the credit. The time I cheated. The time I added to the gossip. The time I deceived another. The time I pretended I didn't know. All those actions that I justified, rationalized, canonized. All those times that the "Beast" within came out to play. Pick up the graphite scalpel and scratch them into life.

"I knew that he was trying to help, but I hated his success. I said just enough to let people doubt him. I used his confidence to humiliate him. I felt an evil comfort seeing him fall."

"I waited until I knew no one could see. I kicked the door just as he stepped up to open it. I used it to hurt him. I wanted him to cry."

"I pretended I didn't care. I knew that he needed my support. I steeled myself against him. I felt powerful when I watched him suffer."

"I lied when I told my wife that I was meeting with people after work. I spent the time nurturing another relationship. I told myself I needed to feel better. I repressed my guilt."

Can clean water flow from polluted springs? I catalogue my behavior. I could tell myself that there are plenty of offsetting good actions. I have been kind. I have been generous. Sometimes I've loved without recompense. I have offered help. All of this is true, but it is only half the truth. I have lied. I have cheated. I have rejected others and God. I have used others for my own gains. I have hated. I have sought revenge. I have debased others. I've done damage. That is the other truth. The truth I will not face. The truth that I am sick.

These two truths war inside me. I am not free to be what I want to be because I find the disease drives me to be what I don't want to be. A submarine under the ocean of evil waters, I find my hull is leaking. As I close one pressure door after another, the evil spreads deeper and deeper into my sanctuary. Its weight overcomes my balance. I sink.

Prognosis

When a submarine falls too deeply within the ocean, it implodes. The outside pressure can no longer be resisted by the man-made shell protecting the life within. The steel itself collapses. The hull rushes inward, crushing everything.

I am submerged. The waters of living have closed around me. I breathe recycled air. I am alive but I cannot stop the pressure leaks. The outside pushes in, harder and harder as I drop into the depths. Soon I will die in an inward collapse. I will be crushed by my outward reality. The weight of guilt, shame, deceit, envy, pride, antagonism—it must reach equilibrium. There are only two solutions. I will continue to fall until the pressure from the outside is balanced on the inside by crushing my protective shell and flooding my existence with its dark, cold water. Or I must rise to the surface, reduce the outside imbalance and find fresh air.

Submarines navigate under water through instruments designed to tell the captain vitally important information. Information necessary to life itself. How deep am I? Am I going up or down? How long have I been here? But I am submersed with instruments that are unreliable. I don't know if I am going up or down. I can't tell how deep I am. I have no confidence in the measure of how long I have been here. I can't trust myself. Just like a submarine without instruments, only one reality is certain. Gravity will pull me down. The illness will spread.

Directions

My pencil and paper list is getting long. It is made up of a life-time of small hurts and large transgressions. None of them are trivial. Nothing trivial is remembered. The paper in my lap weighs upon me. The agony of putting down another line. The shame, the ugliness of my life of self-deceit. It is an obituary to myself, all the remembrances never spoken at the grave. A map of where I have been. A sign of where I am going.

Directions. "How do you get there from here?" "Just keep going and you can't miss it." I started on my road many years ago. Without paying attention, I passed lots of yellow signs. Warning signs. Danger signs. Then I ran a few stop signs. Right through the red zone. I lived. I went faster. "I know this road," I would tell myself. It's the yellow brick road. To paradise. To happiness. To peace. Wherever I longed to go, this road would take me there. I believed in the pavement of fool's gold.

One day I looked out the passenger window and realized that the landscape was passing by so fast I could no longer see it. Red and yellow, black and white became a stream of gray. Then I knew what I had always forgotten. The yellow brick road was the road to destruction. But now I couldn't get off.

A one-word description. Remember. One word that says who we *feel* that we are. Don't trust yourself to put down who you *think* you are. Your thinking will lie to you. Who we think we are is just too unreliable because it is influenced by our excuses. We need the harsh reality of our behavior to modify the thought reality of our excuses. Look at that list. What is the word?

Drunk. Addict. Hater. Resentful. Power-hungry. Adulterer. Envious. Lustful. Compulsive. Thief.

Liar. Vengeful. There's a long list of possibilities. My mind wants to say, "But these are all negatives. I'm good too!" That is my broken navigation instrument talking. Reality is all that pressure on the outside trying to break in. Lonely. Fearful. Guilty. Prideful. One word that names the disease. The disease that will not go away. Without a name, there is no cure. Without a name, every direction is down. Find a word for my sickness. Face myself and name the beast! There will be plenty of time to remember all the good things that we are but the crisis of this cancer can't wait. I can't get well if I won't face my disease. That must come first.

How Well Am I?

Before you decide that you have already had enough religious incantations perpetrated upon you in your short life, ask some self-examination questions. Determine for yourself whether you are ill. And if you find that you are (for only you can know for sure), then commit yourself to this exercise in recovery. You have nothing to lose and perhaps your life to gain.

Ten TRUE or FALSE questions. Ruthless honesty please. Why pretend, no one is looking?

1. The people in my life who matter most to me really understand who I am. They love me regardless of anything that I have done. I feel completely open with them.

2. I feel truly free.

3. I have completely forgiven all those who have intentionally or unintentionally injured or disappointed me over the years.

4. My conscience is clear and I have a positive sense of well-being about those actions that I deliberately or accidentally took in the past that harmed or mistreated myself or others. I have completely forgiven myself.

5. I awake each day with a renewed sense of purpose and celebration for the life that I lead.

6. I know that I am cared for, that my very existence is part of a greater, living pattern.

7. I know what it means to love and be loved, and I am presently immersed in this deep understanding. Life is joyful for me.

8. I welcome the responsibilities I have chosen for my life, knowing that they serve a higher purpose no matter how trivial they may seem at the moment. I am content.

9. My struggles with fear, anxiety, guilt, pride, anger and/or despair are passing emotions that I am able to surrender to the greater purpose I enjoy.

10. I am not afraid to die.

Did any question uncover concern? Disharmony? Shame? Did any question cry out for resolution? Only our secret selves can know. But a single FALSE answer is a start. The disease is deadly. It is so lethal that it deliberately disguises itself by

13

altering our awareness of it. These simple questions will provide a small dose of shock treatment. Get us awake. Prod us forward.

Time for some serious examination.

CHAPTER TWO

The Beast

When I kept silent about my sin, my body wasted away through my groaning all day long. For day and night Thy hand was heavy upon me; My vitality was drained away as with the fever-heat of summer. (Psalm 32:3-4)

Wretched man that I am! Who will set me free from this body of death? (Romans 7:24)

"I just don't know what came over me. I didn't mean it."

"I'm sorry. What can I say? That's not who I am."

"It was like looking in from the outside and watching me do things I never could have imagined I would do. I can't believe that I did those things even now, but I know that it's true."

There is a beast in each of us. Something alien, crouching in the dark parts of our being, waiting for the moment of anger, or passion, or pretense to leap into the light. To lurch from within us and make us into something we thought we were not. Awful. Ugly. Evil.

Denial to cover it up. Shame to protect it. Hate to pacify it. Anger to feed it. Unwanted behavior to forget it. But we never get free of it. Each time the beast breathes the breath of our lungs, its power grows. Each time we push it back into our secret recesses, it clamors for more room. The cage shakes, the bars break and out it comes, seeking revenge for our denial of its grip on us. Driving us to our personal hell, we are propelled into another round of drinking or drugs, sex or violence, eating, envy, revenge, arrogance, resentment, disappointment.

"Wait just a minute," you say. "I'm not like that. I've never had an affair. I don't curse and swear. I treat everyone with respect. I keep my temper under control. I don't drink, smoke or do drugs. You can't be talking about me."

Dark Hallways

But I am talking about you – and about me. Every one of us has dark hallways. Inside the corridors of our minds there are those places where the light switches have been deliberately turned off. That's where we find the lair of the beast. That little bit of envy, that silent rage, that secret need for power, that fleeting thought of revenge, that sudden wish for violence, that daydream of desire. It's all there, isn't it? Whitewashed on the outside, rotting on the inside. Just underneath the lid held tightly in place.

These are not closets. Closets have containment doors. We are well practiced at keeping closet doors shut. We know the shame of being found with a closet door open. These are not closets. They are passages – tunnels – dark hallways. They lead us from room to room. But as soon as we step into these hallways, we can never find the way back to the entrance. All we can do is move from one exit to the next—always down, deeper and deeper—to meet the Beast.

"I can't imagine what this is all about," you say (but the hair on the back of your neck is already starting to feel the fear of disclosure). "I have never been led into a dark inner place," you protest (but your heart is pounding just a little bit louder). Let's do a little dungeon exploration. Take my hand and I will show you just one of these hallways, but hold on tight for it's very easy to get lost in here.

The entrance to this dark hallway carries the sign, "Loneliness." It's a pleasant enough sounding excuse for many manifestations of the Beast. After all, we tell ourselves, no one should have to be lonely. What we need is companionship. What we get is heartache. The dark hallway we travel to get there is sex. Everyone knows love's ashes. Sometime, somewhere the fire of passion was extinguished. It did not just go out. It was put out. Not enough fuel (too little understanding), not enough heat (too great expectations), not enough oxygen (too little communication) and out it went. You and I stood there empty. Burned. Ashes. The Beast in us filed away a memory-wound to use another day. It was a wound that would make us just a little less vulnerable, a little more cautious, a little more skeptical the next time. And, of course, wounds cause infection.

So the next time love presented itself to us, we remembered the wound. We remembered and we infected the new relationship with the hurts of the past. Spontaneity was displaced by wariness, exuberance was reduced to circumspection, truth was modified to advantage. The Beast prepared us for another pound of soot by equipping us to fulfill our own nightmare of disappointment. The more we tried to maneuver away from any risk of pain, the more pain's razor edge cut our souls. When we lost enough blood, we ended it, justified because we held ashes in our hands. Our purity was mixed with poison. The beautiful apple that we wanted looked so delicious, but it was meant to kill.

This hallway leads us from disappointment to resignation. If we could not be loved without conditions, then we would have conditions for our loving. Relationships became contracts. We bargained for the companionship we sought by trading what we had for what we thought we could get. Minds for power, platitudes for intimacy, peace for presence. In the end, it was only a board game with plastic players. Partners were interchangeable weapons used to fight against the creeping darkness inside. The Beast was having his way, invading our light at a faster and faster pace. Every new contract reinforced our essential lovelessness. The only way out was down.

The next exit was lit by a neon sign, "Please yourself." The ultimate escape. When the world is filled with risk-avoidance, loving encounters lose meaning. Love and sex coexist in confused disharmony. Sex is nothing more than the use of a lobotomized orifice for self-flagellation. "This space for rent - make offer." Despair drives us to **seek** the Beast. What we fled before we now embrace. We practice the art of anesthesia in auto-eroticism. Endorphins replace emptiness. The soul sinks while the body performs a ritual of *angst* relief. The end is inevitable, left alone in the darkness of our own shame.

Of course, you and I are like this. We are human. We are battered, bruised, beaten beings. We have known pain, disappointment, agony, emptiness because we are alive. That is all it takes. Just living. And because just living can be such hell, we let the Beast take control. We batter others with the hands of the Beast. We cheat others with the heart of the Beast. We lie to others with the mouth of the Beast. We manipulate, malign and masturbate with the mind of the Beast. We dress in human skin to fool our victims. But underneath that living flesh is an alien seeking revenge on an unaccepting world. We die; it lives.

Why can't the alcoholic stop drinking? Why can't the druggie stop shooting up? Why can't the sex addict stop lusting? Why can't the embittered stop shouting? Why can't the fearful stop crying? Why can't the abused stop hitting? Can it be that there is any pleasure left in the drink, or the drugs, or the orgasm, the screaming, the tears, the violence? No, a thousand times, no. The real pleasure is gone. What is left is only numbing the pain. There is no peace, comfort or harmony in these things. That has all been extracted through instinctual repetition. There is only self-destruction, self-defeat, self-addiction. Every occurrence reinforces the strangle hold of the Beast. Every repetition removes more of my freedom. I am chained to the Beast, a living schizophrenic, a dying parasite.

The Spiral Staircase

Once more you protest. "Yes, it's true that I have felt disappointment," you say. "I have been hurt. I have been scared. But I'm over that. I have learned to control my feelings. You see. I don't drink. I don't screw around. I'm not like this thing you're talking about. I've learned to handle my own problems."

You're absolutely right. You are not an alcoholic, a drug user, a sex addict, an abuser, a hater, a pleasure seeker. **Not yet.** You're still traveling. You just haven't arrived at the last exit. You haven't played the End Game. **But you will.** Because the Beast is alive in you. You have let him have a small space in your heart and he will never rest until he owns it all. You can fight him all your life, but in the end, he will win no matter what you do. You can't win the fight against this cancer because the Beast has the ultimate weapon. The Beast owns death.

This is so important and so dangerous. The great lie of the Beast is the lie of shame. No matter how seemingly insignificant our sin, we open the cage of the Beast when we allow the guilt that we feel to press our transgression into the dark recesses. King David made it very clear. "When I kept silent about my sin, my body wasted away through my groaning all day long." Hiding my sin feeds the Beast. It begins with the fear of rejection. If they only knew what I did, they could not love me. Somehow, we think that we can be loved if we hide our shame. But we soon find that just the opposite is true.

Since others continue to act as though they love me, I now conclude that they love me precisely because they do not know my guilt. But I know. So I stop loving me. And the result is that I must stop loving them, for I know that I am a sham. God comes next. Perhaps He was really first in this bestial logic. God does know. And since He knows my guilt, He also knows that I have denied my guilt. I hate myself for denying my guilt because by denying my guilt, I pretend to be someone I am not. I am forced to live a lie, to love a lie. And that I cannot do. So, my hatred for the self I am, but do not want to be, is extended to God. I cannot let God see my guilt. I am ashamed. God could never love me because I can never love me. A bestial tautology. Love and lies cannot coexist.

We need to be careful not to think that bestial struggles are only for those who have corrupting behavior. It would be easy to say that alcoholics and drug users, child abusers and rapists, haters, hedonists and those of that caliber are candidates for the Beast, but not me. Actually, the Beast doesn't care what baits the trap. It could just as easily be the pleasure of eating, the thrill of shopping, the extra adrenaline of competition. It can be as trivial as potato chips and coffee, television or sunbathing. The Beast can set the trap with the attraction of money or the aversion of airplanes.[2] He doesn't care what the bait is, as long as it works. When we

---

[2] Compare the attraction and aversion addictions listed in Gerald May, *Addiction and Grace*, Harper & Row, 1988, pp. 38-39 for a very enlightening experience.

confront the Beast, we confront an enemy who can use punishment or reward with equal alacrity.

The Beast breathes the air of shame. Shame isolates me from the forgiveness of others. It separates me from the community of the guilty. It convinces me that I alone am unworthy of love. <u>Shame is the dark power of the Beast</u>. A power so great that I feel its slow strangulation every waking moment, until finally I must kill that thing I hate – me. Every unconfessed sin contains within it the mark of the Beast. Every unconfessed sin has the potential of shackling us to the power of shame and driving us to embrace the horror of the Beast.

Are you frightened enough to really look into that hallway? Have you seen him behind your bathroom mirror? Did you feel his presence when you last were angry, or lonely, or hurt? If we choose to deny him, he wins. He loves that shadow world, the world we can't look at because of our shame. The more darkness we hold inside, the greater power we give to the Beast. To stay human, we must kick down the doors, open the windows, turn on the floodlights and let our parasites show. If we want to be human, we must expose the Beast inside us.

What a terrible specter that is – to let another know my secret shame. The fear immobilizes me. Panic floods my soul. To let someone else see the me that even I do not want to know that I am. It is almost too much to bear. This is the crux of our problem. We not only lack the power to fight the creature who is us, we lack the desire. We let the Beast live in us **because we want to.** The operations of the Beast numb us to the disappointments of reality. In order to kill the Beast, we would have to stop pretending that the world should treat us fairly. We would have to stop pretending that we should have things our way. We would have to stop pretending that we deserve comfort when we are hurt. We would have to face our naked selves without excuses. The Beast is alive because we would rather live with myth than with reality. Reality is harsh, unforgiving and remorseless. Anything could happen to us. Anything at all. When those things happen that take away our sense of wellbeing, that strip us of our pride, our self-respect, our love of ourselves, we uncage the Beast to **protect us.** We turn the Beast loose on our perceived enemies whether they be other people or the cold impersonal world itself. And the Beast responds. The Beast always comforts us by anesthetizing our pain and shifting our blame.

Bestial Logic

Avarice, anger, drunkenness, drugs, sex, violence, pleasure, hate. Bestial actions all do two very important things. First, they numb our pain either by helping us forget or by focusing our energy on some outside enemy. Secondly, they reconstitute our loss of power. I drink to forget. I also drink to take control of my hurt. If I lash out in anger, if I shout, scream or verbally batter another, the energy output numbs my own sense of hurt. At the same time, it re-establishes my personal power through my ability to be vengeful, hateful or violent.

Numbing and powerlessness go together. My experience of pain, my encounter with disappointment is a failure of power. I have not been able to control my world in such a way that I was rewarded by the successful culmination of my desires. I failed. Something or someone got the upper hand and I was hurt. My power is threatened. So the Beast rushes to my aid at precisely the point where I am most needy. In the panic of a threat to personal power, I need to forget the failure and reconnect with the belief that I am in control. The strength of the Beast is its ability to fulfill these two psycho-emotive needs.

Now we see why we can't fight the Beast and hope to win. We can't fight because we are caught in a vicious circle. We are committed to personal power. That commitment means we inevitably suffer hurt and disappointment which threatens to destroy our personal power. If we try to live without the Beast, but keep our basic commitment to power, we commit psychological suicide. We have nothing to protect us. We are victimized. But if we try to live with the Beast and wish to maintain that commitment to personal power, we will have to let the Beast have greater and greater control of who we are each time we confront pain. To live in the world is to live in a wilderness, full of hurts and pains and fears, surrounded by hideous creatures and unimaginable traumas. In an effort to shore up our finitude in this vast wilderness, we succumb to the myth of power; the myth that power will protect us from the contingencies of life. Buried in that myth is the denial of death. The myth of power denies the reality of death. The Beast feeds us a diet pungent with the aroma of victory, victory over puny selves, victory over our feeble enemies, victory over our intransigent world. And while we eat, the Beast keeps us alive, focused on the fable of destiny, convincing us that we too can be a god.

Death and Life

The truth is something very different. The truth is that I can only pretend to escape death if I become something other than human. The truth is that humanness depends entirely on dying. The more that I push against the maelstrom of death, the more I am forced to give away my humanness. And this is precisely the strategy of the Beast. "Give me your wounds, and I will avenge them," says the Beast. But the price we pay is to forsake forgiveness. Something human must die to feed the power need. "Give me your sorrows and I will erase them." But we must pay the price of numbing reality. "Give me your depression, your disappointment, your despair and I will turn it into cold, hard power." But we pay the price of turning from God's comfort, peace and joy to something made by inhuman hands.

To follow the path of the Beast is only to delay the inevitable. That delay is extremely appealing. The path of the Beast claims to reinstate our divinity. The Beast promises us control. We believe that we can have the world perform according to our wishes either because we will force it to act appropriately or we will deny its intransigence and create our own cosmos. The Beast transforms our pain into the delusion of power or the mythology of fantasy. And in that moment, it seems as though the promise of the Beast is fulfilled. I can make others perform according to my wishes. I know the power of manipulation, threat and violence. I can enlist the

Beast's ownership of death to create fear in another. I can get what I want. And if I am not successful, if I do not have enough power, I can forget. The Beast will bring me any number of pain killers. I can reduce myself to anesthetized existence. Either way, the pain will stop for a moment. Either way I will become instinctual, Beast-like. Either way I will take a step away from being human.

There is no escape. To destroy the grip of the Beast on my life, I must first confront my commitment to control. Here we find the subtle toxin of the Beast. The Beast has a grip on me because I cannot be God. Only God has the power to order life in such a way that His desires are fulfilled. Only God can create a world in which justice and mercy reign. In spite of all of our attempts to the contrary, we cannot be God. We cannot re-create the world to fit our desires. We cannot insure that the world will operate in perfect harmony for us. To add insult to injury, we will die. The ultimate statement of our finitude is fixed for every one of us. Death comes calling. **The truth about life is death**, but no one committed to the need for control is willing to face this truth. The Beast accommodates our desire to be self-deluded.

This metaphysical explanation uncovers the depth of our problem, but it seems so removed from our ordinary experience. We deal in the insignificant trivialities of life, not in the musing of the great philosophers. What has the denial of our finitude, the denial of death got to do with driving to work, changing diapers, looking for a parking place or answering the telephone? A simple story will show the connection between ordinary, everyday and the desire for divine control.

A Definition

Addiction is a habitual neurophysiological mismanagement of emotional trauma.

The Morning After

The day starts with surrender. When the alarm goes off, we remind ourselves that this is the day that the Lord has made, and we should be glad in it. But the three-year-old got up at 2:45 AM and cried until we also got up for the 25 minutes needed to get him back to sleep. And we didn't get to bed early because there was some family trouble back on the West Coast, so the telephone was busy until 11PM. When the alarm goes off, we really don't want to get up yet. Say a little prayer for the day while trying to catch a few more minutes of rest. Then the eyes snap open and we are already behind schedule. No time for a Psalm now. To the shower, the closet and out the door. Breakfast was a glass of orange juice somewhere in between shoes and coat. Just as the door to the car closed, we remember that we need gas. A few more minutes shot. Down to the station, but the lines are long and facing the wrong way. So we make a quick U-turn and find that someone else has pulled into the spot we were targeting. A small exclamation of disgust leaves the lips. Then the simmer of frustration while we wait. "Come on, come on." Patience is not a virtue when you have to wait for it. Finally, the gas pump. Out to the freeway, but (Oh, no!) an accident. More simmering. Forget that someone else will be permanently late. What matters most is that we are inconvenienced. "They ought to have a law," comes the phrase as we see that a truck has overturned in the fast lane. Finally, at work. The parking garage. A car appears in our reserved spot. That does it! Out comes the notepad, a short memo on the virtues of minding the rules slapped on the windshield, accompanied by a threat if it happens again. "Doesn't anyone know who I am around here?" The cry for control!

The other half has an equally trivial day. The three-year-old refuses to eat breakfast and decides that none of the correct clothes are worth wearing. There is a battle of wills over which pair of shoes will go to pre-school. Tears in the car about wanting cereal instead of a sandwich. Harsh words (justifiable!?) over wearing a seat belt. "Why me?" echoes in the mind. From the pre-school blitz to the gym. The locker room is too cold. The locker door closes on a new shirt stamping an insignia in grease. At least the workout doesn't result in an injury. Shopping. The advertised special is out. Rain check line. There aren't enough bag boys. Writing checks and packing your own groceries. "Why don't they do something about how they treat customers?" In the car suddenly remembering the forgotten purchase of the birthday present. Pre-school birthdays, a pain for everyone except the kids. Back to the store. More waiting. Finally home, unpacking and then the telephone. Ring! a MasterCard offer. Hang up. Ring! just buy 6 weeks and... Hang up. Ring! pre-school, the child is sick, you'll have to come and get him. "God, be merciful to me, a mother!" "Why can't the world be the way that I want it to be?" Control! Eat a chocolate bar to feel better.

Power and Control

In our little drama of a work day morning, we talked about control. We made a distinction between the power of God and the human desire for control. This distinction is important and often confused. Our world is full of symbols of control. The epitome of our role models is typically a control figure. Thus, the President, the Chief Executive, the Policemen, the Teacher, the Parent are all seen as representatives of authority and power, but the truth is that they are, more often than not, symbols of social agreement to standards of control. They exercise their power not because they are personally powerful but because they are perceived as ones who have the right of authority. When the social agreement collapses, the power disappears. This is not necessarily socially disturbing. The passage of one administration to another means that a new President receives the collective social agreement as a symbol of authority. The old President no longer has this power, but it would be unjustified to say that the old President is no longer the same person because he no longer has the social contract to be the authority figure.

When the police lose control of a situation, it is not because they have individually lost some power. The social contract to recognize them as authority symbols has changed. On large scale, this is the basis for revolution. Every parent knows the feeling of loss of control when confronted by the collapse of the social contract with teenage children. These situations help us see that what we typically call power is really the application of control through advantage or leverage. The power of the boss is really his leverage over my work agreement. Difficult employees are difficult precisely because they do not recognize this control. The power of the parent or the government works exactly the same way. Each has leverage or advantage over its subjects. This is control.

Janet Hagberg has catalogued the progressive stages of power in her book, *Real Power*[3]. She describes six stages from powerlessness to power by gestalt. She notes that our society generally rewards stages that define power by association, symbols or reflection. On reflection, we might ask how these stages differ from control behavior. Only Hagberg's Stage Six (power by gestalt) seems to transcend issues of control. Power by gestalt has the following characteristics:

> comfortable with paradox, unafraid of death, powerless, quiet in service, ethical, on the universal plane[4]

Stage Six individuals do not fit well into society. They seem to operate on an altogether different plane, with a personal vision that directs their lives without regard to the social contract. Hagberg says that they are "powerless", but what we really see is that they have given up the myth of control. They

---

[3]Janet O. Hagberg, *Real Power: Stages of Personal Power in Organizations* (Harper & Row, San Francisco), 1984.
[4]Hagberg, p. 147.

are true examples of **power** precisely because they understand that they are not in control, of their lives or of anything else. The reason that we call them powerless is because we do not recognize the difference between power and control.[5] They do not easily fit our paradigm.

What, then, is power? We are not interested in the application of the term to the inanimate world except as those applications help us understand the principle area of our concern. Therefore, what we really want to know is how does the term "power" apply to human beings? What do we mean when we say that this human being has power? Hagberg's insight that personal power which emanates from within has the appearance of being powerless (Stage Six) helps us see that we must remove the control and controlling issues from our understanding. That means that true power will not come from the consensus of social agreement. <u>True power is not a function of control.</u> That does not mean that individuals who exhibit true power will not have tremendous influence on the rest of us. It simply means that their influence will not be a matter of social position, agreement or advantage. They will exert influence because they empower others, not because they control others. One who is powerless (in the current paradigm) cannot control.

---

[5]Hagberg has a very telling comment when she raises the question about a seventh stage. She says, "I have a strong suspicion that there is a Stage Seven in this model of personal power. I have deliberately chosen not to describe the stage, probably because I had enough trouble describing people at Stage Six. My sense is that it would be called something like Power by Transcendence and that the crisis to overcome in order to reach it would be the crisis of being human." (p. 148)

There is only one framework which reveals the true meaning of power. That framework is the interplay between Man and God. The roots of our civilization recognized the sacred quality of real power in the Greek use of the term *dynamai*. The fundamental purpose of power for the Greeks was to align the cosmic forces for good and evil in order to escape the tragic consequences of the human condition. Power was couched in religion and dealt with the primary concern of religion - the fact of death. Men did not have power, they were only capable of sharing in the power resident in the divinities of the cosmos. But sharing that power was the only way that men could escape the tragedy of being both spirit and body.

It is but a short step from the notion of sharing the power of the cosmos to protect oneself from the inevitability of decay and death to the belief that power is to be found in controlling the cosmos. In some ways, the entire history of Western civilization is nothing more than the application of technology in pursuit of control of chaotic forces. The dark underworld of the body must be forced into submission through the application of technology of the mind. Death, the final chaos, is apparently kept at bay.

Once we recognize that power is intimately connected with the sacred, we must look at the other roots of our tradition to see how their influence modified this Greek quest. The Judeo-Christian use of power is also pre-eminently religious. But there is a very big difference. Where Greek thought was built on the dualism of body and spirit, the Jewish background had no such dualism. Overcoming the tragic condition of Mankind was not an issue of subduing a chaotic creation or a decaying material existence. God created both the natural order and Man. And both were pronounced good. The issue which confronts power from the Jewish perspective is not the chthonic chaos but the deliberate disobedience of Mankind. It is not a matter of primeval disharmony but of destroyed relationship. What stands behind power is not a share of the divinity of the natural forces but the righteous will of a personal Creator. This changes the whole picture. Power is not a function of control because power is, first and foremost, a function of righteousness; that is to say, it is the result of a personal right standing before one's own Creator. Thus, it automatically excludes any extension to advantage, leverage or control. To stand before one's Creator is to recognize unconditional powerlessness. It is to acknowledge absolute dependence. It is to be overwhelmed by one's misalignment with the true holiness of the Source of all being. Defying death is not an issue at all. In the face of the Creator God there is no such thing as death. There is only life with or without righteousness.

The Judeo-Christian tradition places power in its proper context. That context shows us that real power must belong to the sphere of inner holiness, that the energy of real power influences men precisely because it calls them to self-examination in relation to their own right standing before the Creator. It can never be control by social contract, force, conscription or any mental or physical means. Real power is of an entirely different nature – it originates with God and expresses itself in men through humility, sacrifice, acceptance and obedience.

Hagberg describes the sixth stage as a stage where individuals no longer fear death. Now we see that there are obvious reasons for this. The shared power which emanates from the Creator God is a power that has broken the control of death over Mankind. There is no need to fear death if one is aligned with God. The issues for those who share in the endowment of real power are not issues of the Greek struggle against chaos. They are issues of the struggle against sin and they can only be fought in the arena of weakness. To exhibit real power is to reveal the God of weakness. No wonder the world cannot accommodate such people into its paradigm of control. The world does not share the same universe.

Power and Fantasy

Real power is of divine origin. It shows itself in the humility of acceptance, the integrity of inner peace, the absence of fear and the complete human helplessness of divine dependence. Real power is as alien to our way of thinking and behaving as conversations among animals. We can imagine that such things exist, but we can do so only by forcing their presence into our mold of the world. The challenge and the call of real power compels us to return to our own origin – to re-establish our relationship with the divine and to become partakers in that energy. Real power can never be humanly generated. It can only empower us to become truly human.

In contrast, the power that we recognize as control is not sacred in its origin. It is thoroughly man-made. As a result, the power of control has its origin in the principles which govern the world order apart from God. Theologically, this form of power is the bastardization of the divine. It denies the dependence of creation on the Creator. It seeks to manipulate the world from the perspective of the active agent, the human being wishing to exercise control. Does this mean that all control power is inappropriate (or worse, sinful)? The answer must be a resounding, "No!" There is a place for the exercise of authority. Even God demonstrates such power and provides for control power as an extension of the divine will. But control power can never be an end in itself. Power for the sake of control is not human. It is bestial. It is based on my need to become god, to block my pain, to force reality to meet my needs. Insofar as it separates me from my right-standing relationship with the true source of all power, it undermines my own humanness.

In the world as it is, the exercise of control power is the accepted medium of interaction. In spite of our recognition that our relationships are not what we want them to be, because of the struggle of each party over control, we steadfastly refuse to see that the relationship fails to meet our expectations not because we do not have the right mechanics of shared control but because control power is antithetical to real relationships. Control power must depend on advantage. But real relationships can only flourish in an atmosphere of self-sacrifice, that is in precisely the atmosphere where control has no advantage. Relationships with our friends, work peers, spouses and children disintegrate to the degree that we attempt to apply control power instead of sharing enabling power. This is no accident. It is simply a reflection of the relationship we have with ourselves and with God. The more that we attempt to control either self or God, the less satisfying and successful the relationship becomes. Real power is an endowment of divine energy, initiated from position of weakness. Only real power is capable of overcoming the control of the Beast because only real power removes the threat that the Beast uses for advantage. The weakness of real power refuses to allow the Beast a stronghold of shame, because such weakness offers no excuse for its own condition. It is helpless and admits it. The dependence of real power casts aside the final weapon of the Beast because Death is no longer a priority issue.

There is a theological expression for the condition of experiencing real power. It is called grace. Grace is the biblical expression for sharing the endowment of real power. Grace is concerned not with control but with recovery. The God of grace is interested in the restitution of a relationship of right standing, that is, in the recovery of true humanness through a return to the intended sacred fellowship between Man and Creator God. This can only come about through the confrontation and confession of Man's illegitimate rebellion. Grace is the result of repentance. Grace is not a once-for-all action. Grace is a living openness to God. To be a believer is to live grace-fully, to be in a constant state of confession and repentance. Why is this so essential? Because the power of the Beast lies in the darkness of the unconfessed. Shame is *nothing more* than the accumulated guilt of unconfessed sin. But what control this "*nothing more*" exercises.

Why is control power bestial rather than human? The answer lies in the concept of freedom. The Beast would have us believe that freedom is the same as license. For the Beast, freedom is a corollary of power. If I have enough control, I can do what I want. If I have enough power, I have license to do anything. "Look at God," whispers the Beast. "Is there anything that God cannot do? He is all powerful. Therefore, He is free to do whatever he wants. That is real freedom. To be uninhibited in the expression of my desires. To be in control." And if I experience my finitude as frustration of my power, the Beast comforts me with the freedom of fantasy. "It's true that you can't always get what you want," he says. "At least in this world. But there is another world, a world inside, where you can be anything, do anything. Where no one can stop you. Numb the real world and live in your dreams. Be free."

This is the freedom of a condemned prisoner. The reality of his existence is that he is already dead. It is just a matter of time. He is already an erased person, but at the moment it does not appear so. The prisoner can move about in the cell. He can contemplate, converse and commiserate. He can imagine that reality is something other than the four concrete walls. He can vent his frustration and anger. What he cannot do is escape. Every time the instinctual reactions of the Beast find expression in our lives, the chains that bind us to this ironic freedom grow a little heavier. The Beast succeeds by deliberately confusing control and power.

We need to be very clear about the meaning of freedom. Freedom is not a word that was invented in the me-generation. It has nothing to do with facilitating my desires. What we like to call "freedom" when we think that we choose to participate in our special addictions to power and fantasy is actually the opposite of freedom. Addictions do not free us; they enslave us. The addictions of the Beast make us captive to the mythology that we can have the world our way. When we indulge ourselves in this myth, we experience counterfeit freedom just as we exhibit counterfeit power.

Control power moves in the opposite direction of freedom. From control, I can only derive compulsion. Bestial (counterfeit) freedom closes the possibilities of encounter by restricting my openness to alternatives. The commitment to control narrows my focus, centers attention on me, on my needs and desires. Every time this occurs, I limit the social, physical and spiritual interactions that *could* occur. The result is that my world becomes smaller, my options fewer. With fewer options come limited choices, until finally, the hallmark characteristic of humanness can no longer be expressed. When I act as the Beast, I act not on choice but on instinct. My pathways have been prescribed. I become a determined being.

The Beast would have me believe that this power will rescue me from pain, that I can exercise my freedom to deliver me from my wilderness. The

Beast lives on that basis that survival requires self-protection and self-aggression – that I must fight the world and others for my right to be – that I must be in control. But control does not lead me to peace. It does not draw me to responsibility. It does not offer me consolation or love. Control power depends entirely on advantage and **advantage is entirely relative**. Control requires a Master-Slave relationship. Control removes any hope of grace. Nietzsche's *Will to Power* is not an expression of human being. It is an expression of animal dominance. Human beings cannot live by control power because, in the words of Bob Dylan, "You gotta serve somebody." No one is ultimately in control except God and His control does not stem from advantage but from holiness. The great irony is this: If human beings try to live life according to control alone, they become living examples of the law of the jungle. They become animals, creatures driven by instinctual logic, who are ultimately not in control at all.

Freedom and Obligation

True freedom pushes me toward greater openness because true freedom leads me toward the truth. When I experience true freedom, I find that my possibilities for action multiply, not because I have license to do as I please but because I understand the interconnectedness of my choices for the existence of other beings and my ultimate powerlessness. My field is no longer narrowly defined by the instinctual needs of self. I see that every choice which I may make contains within it a myriad of obligations. "Free to do as I please" is an oxymoron for I am never free when I act as I please.

I can only be free when I am pleased to act in ways that strengthen my obligations and are the result of my own sense of dependence.

Real freedom is our capacity to be **bound**, directed and obligated by what we encounter. It is not something that we can earn, nor is it a possession that we can grasp. It is rather a willingness to be indebted to the truth. The authentication of humanness that we long to experience, that sense that we are truly important and loved, cannot be won, forced, cajoled or bargained. Any application of control power used to coerce love destroys love. Freedom moves me away from control, toward dependence. The exercise of freedom puts me in a relationship of reliance on another. Only dependence can verify my worth because only dependence can involve acceptance. To be free is to be accepted as I truly am—powerless and dependent. To be free is to embrace reality without excuse – to love my finiteness for what it is, an expression of my relationship to my Creator, and to revel in the mystery of my being.

Freedom cannot be dislodged from life. I do not exist in the vacuum of bestial instinct even if I choose to pretend that I do. The resistance of the world to my will is nothing more nor less than the refusal of my existential dependence to give way to bestial reality. The will to power is an attempt to fight the real nature of my being. Freedom entails obligation because life entails dependence. I cannot be truly free in a society which requires that my freedom be purchased at the expense of others' slavery, whether that slavery be physical, mental, social or spiritual. Freedom entails obligation because it requires that I extend to other human beings the same valuations of worth which I desire. This can never be true in a society based on control, for control always implies a Master and a Slave. The obligation resident in my freedom expands the responsibility of my choice by enlarging my interconnectedness. It enhances my humanness by reminding me of my finitude. I cannot be deluded by the myth of independence if I am confronted with the infinite ramifications associated with even the smallest of my choices. To be free to choose is to stand in a position of utter dependence - not only for the eventual outcome of my choices but for the very fabric of my existence which allows me to make such choices. Only when I am truly finite can I be truly free. Then, and only then, will I understand and accept that I am not ultimately responsible because I am not and cannot be God. If I am to live at all as a human, it must be by grace. Otherwise, the overwhelming cacophony of my very being will force me to embrace the Beast, to numb my life into instinctual operation, just to survive.

This is the message of freedom found in the Bible. God acts freely to give Man his place in creation. God acts with responsibility and obligation in creating another personal being by establishing interconnectedness as the prerequisite of humanness. Interconnectedness with each other establishes us as human, but it does not end in our obligation to other humans. It extends to God Himself. God created Man to be connected to Him. To be truly free, then, is to stand in a self-aware and self-proclaimed **dependent** relationship with the Creator and the created. That relationship is not to be characterized by the hierarchy of Master and Slave, but by the community of family members – parent and child. That relationship removes the power of bestial logic because it affirms that I matter, even though I am not God, because I matter to God.

The Bible also recognizes that the intended interconnectedness of freedom is not the *modus operandi* of this present world. There is no lack of realism in the Biblical portrayal. Man has given up true freedom for the world of control power. Whether by ignorance, deception or rebellion, we now attempt to create the world based on control; as a result, we are forced to exert inhuman, bestial relationships on creation. We are not willing to let the creation operate on the basis of grace, because we have refused to believe the word of our divine Parent. The final irony is that our efforts to exert control over ourselves and creation, leave us the most out-of-control creatures. Like fish trying to swim on dry land, denying our status as dependent created beings makes us living contradictions. We act as if we are in control but everything around us tells us we are not. This is the result of listening to the fallacious logic of the Beast.

CHAPTER THREE

Prest-o Change-o

The curse of the Beast weighs on me. I want to find the magic cure. To tear this ugly presence from my life. Flush it down the toilet. Away from me. But when I separate even the smallest part of it from me, the empty hole it leaves in my self is so painful that I am soon welcoming it back. The unholy friend is now my blood brother. He simply waits in the shadows for my beckoning to return. It is the addictive despair that I feel. Even though it is a "me" that I have not wanted to admit that I really am, so much of me is in union with this addictive Beast that I cannot feel myself alive without him.

Find the magic cure! Yes, I do want to be rid of this ugliness, but I do not want to be rid of *all* of the Beast. I do want to be free of the guilt, the shame, the destruction of my relationships, my image, my importance. But I don't want to give up my fantasies. I want to escape the fear, the terror, the anxiety. But I don't want to surrender my medication of protection. I want to have the dark recesses of my prison, without the stench of solitary confinement. I need a place where I am no longer confronted with the screaming face, "You're not good enough!"

None of us want the consequences of bestial logic, but we all want the power and protection of the Beast. And that's the catch. The two come together. Always! To become free of my addiction, I must surrender my "control and escape" fantasies. There is absolutely no other way! My own diseased thinking will try to convince me that I can have just a little of each and live with it. But death is death. My diseased thinking will try to tell me that I can keep the consequences under control. But death is still death. And the Beast owns death.

Hard Time

Add one more behavioral fact to our ruthless character assessment. It is a simple question, but the answer is terrifying. "How long has the Beast been alive in my life?" The answer tells me exactly how long I have been feeding our terrible union. The answer tells me how long I have been deceiving myself with bestial logic. The answer tells me how long I have been perfecting my delusion of self-control. The answer tells me how long I have been constructing a prison cell of my own making. And the answer tells me something terrifying. If I have been feeding the Beast for ten, fifteen or twenty years, how long will it take to remove his claws from my soul? Running to the magician for an instant cure is just another pipe dream. There is hard time to be done here—the hard time of recovery.

Why is the grip of the Beast so powerful? Why can't I just let him go? The grip of the Beast is the stranglehold of the shame of secrets. Confusing the difference between power and control leads us to avoid the pain of repentance. It is not easy to confront our real selves much less deliberately expose our shameful animal behavior to God and another human being. As I store up unconfessed sin, I place bricks in the wall of my own prison. I build a cell of solitary confinement. Each brick emphasizes my isolation from God and another human being. Each brick symbolizes my inner shame. Eventually the prison cell that I build around me shuts out the real world altogether. I live in the dark. That, of course, is exactly where the Beast is most at home, where the Beast intends to keep me. The measure of my present state of solitary confinement is simply the degree to which I feel that no one really knows who I am. My isolation is the amount of effort that I put into maintaining the separation between how I appear to others and how I know myself to be. The thickness of my cell walls is determined by my belief that no other being truly cares about me. The paradox is that as much as I want to be known by another and by God, I fear that those who truly know will reject who I am. I want to be loved and I am terrified of the possibility of not being loved, so I pretend in order to be loved, knowing that those who love my pretend self cannot love me as I am *because I won't allow them to see the broken me.*

In the world of bestial logic, there must always be a payback. Whenever I reaffirm my union with the Beast, I pay a price. That price may not be extracted from me during my forays with the Beast. In fact, more often than not, I will find that allowing the Beast to take me for another ride will bring the ecstasy of numbing. I will get another fix. My pain will disappear—but not for long. To get the fix, I will have to pay the price of guilt, shame, remorse, fear and self-loathing. Bestial union is always temporary because the Beast needs me to feel awful so that I will come back for more medication. When I withdraw from the Beast, all of these physical and emotional disturbances increase. I pay the price of withdrawal. And there is always a price.

As impossible as it is for the bestial logic to admit it, God does care. God's ability to send light into my self-made prison is the expression of His love for me while I am in union with the Beast. My response to God's unconditional confirmation that I am loved in spite of my shame, is repentance. *When I repent of even a single attachment to the Beast, I allow God to remove a brick from the wall of my cell.* Light, the light of God that floods reality, bursts into my cell through that single space in the wall. Every time that I act on the basis of God's promise of love for me, another brick falls from my prison cell. More light. I begin to see the world aright. My vision of outer reality is improved with every additional opening. The separation between my inside and my outside begins to close. But every brick that falls increases the risk of rejection and that's the last thing I wish to feel. In this world, rejection is *always possible.* No relationship is guaranteed except the relationship of God's care and concern. I must face the possibility of rejection in order to love and be loved, and the only way I can face this possibility is if I first embrace the God *who will not fail me.* That is easy to write – but very hard to feel, especially when the claws of the Beast are so embedded in my emotional makeup.

Hard time has nothing to do with the appeasement of an angry God. It has nothing to do with paying for my sins. God has already dealt with these issues. God's promise of acceptance and forgiveness does not depend on my penance at all. Hard time is my reality, not God's reality. If we were able to accept all of God's grace toward us in a single moment of time, we would see that the prison walls that kept us locked in solitary confinement are mere chimera, the faintest glimmers of illusion overpowered completely by the intensity of God's love light. But just as the prison around us was built by its own inmate, one brick at a time, so it can only be dismantled one brick at a time. The cell is completely unreal from God's perspective. But from our perspective, we see nothing but the dark shadow that these walls of fantasy cast into our souls. For us, forgiveness happens one day at a time, one act of confession at a time, in spite of the truth that God has flooded all of reality with a bombardment of forgiveness. Either I pay, or God pays, and He is willing even when I am not.

In the solitary confinement cell of my own soul, the Beast slithers to find a dark recess. He waits until the moment comes when I forget that my only reality is to place each brick in the hands of my redeemer. I may even believe that I can tear down the prison walls by myself. But as soon as I tell myself that I can be my own Beast Master, I fall prey to one of those dark corners still left in the prison cell. One day I may decide that I have removed enough bricks. There is plenty of light in my cell. Fresh air pours in through the lattice work I have left in place. In that moment, the Beast simply drags me into one of the remaining dark corners and shuts out the light that I have. I am his again, not because I have replaced the bricks but because I stopped removing them. God's intention is that my inner landscape should perfectly match outer reality. In the outer reality, God is light and in Him is *no darkness at all* (1 John 1:5). If my inner reality is to be conformed to this truth, I will never be finished with the Beast **until every single brick has been torn from the walls.** Hard time is simply the reversal of my building process. God is willing and able to do the demolition work needed to destroy my prison of fantasy. But I am the only one who can offer Him the contract to do so, and I can only offer that contract one brick at a time.

The Jailer

Inmates are not victims in this inner prison. As inmates, we build our own solitary confinement cells. Since the hideous strength of the Beast is the power of this inner darkness, true humanness can only come when the prison walls are gone. That process is a process of active, purposeful surrender; not of will power. Bestial logic performs magic on my will, conscripting my own desires to its aid. I can never break free of the grip of the Beast by my own willpower alone. I must turn to the Jailer for help.

The Jailer holds a key precisely matched to the cell door of my inner prison. Not any key will open this door. It must be a key that is forged so that it fits the unique lock of *my* prison. Since every cell of solitary confinement is as unique as the inmate who occupies it, the key that opens the door to my prison will not be the same one that opens the door to your prison. Fortunately, finding the right key does not matter. The only thing necessary for opening the cell door is to know who the Jailer is.

In every incarceration of solitary confinement, there are four parties, alone together: the Beast, the Inmate, the Jailer and the Redeemer. We know something about the characteristics of the Beast. He cannot live outside the cell, but inside He reigns with life-threatening power. We are really his captives since the walls of the cell belong to him. He assigns us the task of making those walls thicker and thicker as long as we are under his power. Though our cells are self-made over long periods of time, a single brick in the wall casts enough shadow to be a home for the Beast.

We also know the Inmate. Me! You! Caught in the shadow world. Desperate to escape but without the power to do so. Hopelessly chained to the darkness of the Beast. Servants of our own despair. Afraid of the Light that will reveal our bestial selves. Powerless to stop the steady march of bestial dominance.

We know (or at least hope) about the Redeemer. The Biblical record offers us a witness to His mercy. It tells us that God is light. That no darkness is in Him. That He is willing and able to rescue us. That He is where we are—on the inside of our shameful prison. But most of the time, our bestial logic blocks awareness of His presence. In spite of our acknowledgment that God shares this hideous space simply because He is God, our psycho-emotional selves know nothing of God's comforting. Solitary confinement exists because we feel God's absence as much as we feel our own absence. We are alone, no matter who else is there. Knowing that an omnipresent God must be there does not make us free. *Knowing* isn't the problem. It's *feeling* His loving presence that matters.

All of those bricks of guilt, shame and sin will stand forever unless we experience a heart transcendence, a complete reversal of bestial logic. Bestial logic tells us that we are building a prison that has no doors or windows. But bestial logic is wrong. There is a door and the Jailer has the key. The reason that neither the Beast nor the Inmate can see the door is simple: the door does not exist until the Jailer opens it.

How can this be? How can a doorway to the Light be there only when the Jailer decides to open it? And who is this Jailer, the one who knows exactly which key to use but will not use it while we build walls? Answers to these questions come from understanding bestial optics.

Wearing contact lenses provides a useful analogy of bestial optics. When we first put those tiny pieces of plastic into our eyes, they irritate. We could only wear them a few hours at a time. But slowly, imperceptibly, the irritation created calluses on our eyelids. And the calluses numbed the irritation until we no longer could feel the speck in the eye. In fact, the modification of our nervous system feedback was so imperceptible and so effective that we became unaware of the deterioration of the lens from prolonged use. As the lens grows thicker from use, our eye adjusts to the thickness, never notifying us that our vision is gradually becoming distorted. We only realize the distortion exists when we put on brand new lenses and the world is suddenly clearer. In the darkened world of the Beast, our vision of reality becomes progressively distorted. As the light of the outside world is blocked by the walls we create, our ability to distinguish between true and false images fades. In the end, we are convinced that the dark world of the Beast is the real world—the **only** world.

Bestial behavior affects our thinking through imperceptible, insidious alteration of our sensibilities. Because we are subject to progressive bestial blindness, we are blind to another being in our cell. We know that we are in prison and we know that the Beast lives in that prison, but the progressive darkness has made it impossible for us to see that the Jailer is also there. Hold your hand in front of your eyes. Open and close your fingers. The one who holds the unique key needed to unlock the door that does not yet exist has the same hand. There is no magic in seeing this reality. The only thing necessary to see reality is the willingness to look. That hand in your vision is the hand of the Jailer. The Jailer has been here all the time, coexistent with the Inmate, ready to open the door as soon as the Inmate permits him to use the key.

Each of us is in solitary confinement alone together. In our cell is the Beast, the Inmate and the Jailer. They all live in the same person space. The power of darkness, the victimization of guilt and the freedom of repentance—all in the same body. Transformation from one role to the other is a matter of using the key. The Beast in our prison desperately wants us to believe that there is no escape, that dark reality is our only protection. The Inmate is full of doubt, caught between the desire for covering shame and the hope (and fear) of living in the light. The Jailer stands ready, but cannot use the key until the Inmate permits it.

No Inmate can ever use the key. The Inmate is powerless to extricate himself from the clutches of the Beast. The key in his hands is worthless. But the Inmate can *permit* the Jailer to use the key. The Inmate can cast his fate at the feet of the Jailer and admit his powerlessness. He can allow the Jailer to act, not independently of him but with his permission *regardless of the consequences.* This condition is important. There will be consequences for opening the prison cell. Exposure will occur with rescue. Light will flood the present darkness that numbs our sin sensibilities. There will be pain – the pain of shame, guilt and remorse. But it is the pain that heals. No Inmate can enlist the help of the Jailer without these consequences. Life outside will eradicate the hideous comfort of the dark. But once the Inmate is willing to endure the pain that heals to be free from the shackles of the Beast, the Jailer can act.

Using the Key

At this point, most of us will be anticipating the uncomfortableness of "pat" answers. We may feel as though we have been tricked by a sleight of language. In our experience, we have never met the Jailer. We will be suspicious that the key will be another version of one of the following:

1. Moral Management – set realistic goals for self-improvement. Don't beat up on yourself. Take it easy. One step at a time toward a better you. Get control of your life through mental mastery.

2. Religious Reconstruction – acknowledge your sins to God. Bring your life into line with God's morality through devotion to prayer, church and giving. Let go and let God. Promise, penance and purpose.

3. Conscientious Catharsis – reveal your struggles to the therapist, the group or the significant other. Relieve yourself of the burden of being you. Let someone else carry the load. Talk it out. Find linguistic tranquility.

4. Inner Intuition – rediscover your lost wonder. Recognize your hidden divinity. Find a new power within by meditating from without. Initiate your own intrinsic wholeness.

5. Active Accommodation – learn to cope. Live with it instead of fighting it. Rearrange your moral life and loves to accommodate the disharmony. Build stronger defenses for upsetting behavior. Absorb the disease and convert it to positive growth.

Our struggles with the Beast have taught us one very important thing: none of these five self-help promises work. How do we know? Because at one time or another we have tried every one of them, and we still live in the dark. The stench of the Beast still fills our nostrils every time we breathe. The Beast simply does not go away, and any promise that proclaims he will is sheer folly. We cannot live with the Beast but we cannot live without him either. To eradicate the Beast is to destroy me. This is the first terrible consequence of permitting the Jailer to use the key. Once I let the Beast into my life, I will never be free of him as long as I remain on this earth. That is the truth! The first consequence of using the key is to own this truth. The Beast is forever.

I must set aside any mythological hope that somehow the Beast will be taken away from me. Rescue is indeed possible, but it will not come by killing the Beast. That only happens in fairy tales. I may open the door to my cell, but the open door will not cause the cell to evaporate. An open door only means that I may exit or enter. The cell will always be there, a prison without walls, waiting to take me back.

The second consequence of using the key is "son" burn. Using the key exposes me to the Light of God's holiness. No man can stand in this light without burning. If I want to live in the light, I must be prepared to have the years of my dark disease scorched from me. The pain that heals will call me to ask forgiveness, to make amends, to expose my weakness, to risk my soul, to repent, to give up my protection and control. There is no other way to let the light in. I will have to learn *of* the Son of the Most High, and follow his instructions, because he is the only fully human being who ever lived. He knows me.

Does this mean that I am hopelessly trapped? Does this mean that my life will never be what I desire but am unable to produce? What is rescue if the Beast remains? All of these questions are answered when we use the key. Our solitary confinement was brought about by believing that we could control the

Beast. The Beast offered us protection, pleasure and power. We accepted. We wanted his gifts without paying the price. But the price is always right, and when the payment came due, we discovered that the consequences isolated us from the very gifts we thought were our personal nirvana. So we made a deal with the Beast. We played "live and let live." We thought we were in charge. Now we know that we were seduced. The Beast is simply uncontrollable. Relationship with the Beast is the curse of a life **out of control**. Owning my "out-of-control" life is the key that opens the door.

The curse that I so anxiously want to escape is the only thing in my life that constantly causes me to face my true reality. It never lets me forget my powerlessness. It never lets me pretend that I am in charge. It always points me outside myself. It always brings me face-to-face with God. The curse gets me on my knees. My special bestial agony is the one absolutely painful event in my life that will never let me forget who God is and how much I need Him. It is my **sacred curse**.

No wonder I cannot eradicate the Beast. If I were to do so, I would eliminate my dependence on God. It is only in the presence of my *sacred curse* that I recognize my utter helplessness. And God can only rescue me in my absolute weakness.

Twelve Step programs recognize the critical nature of this relationship in two words: "powerlessness" and "surrender." If I believe that I am able, I do not need God and I can't be rescued. If I believe that I am able, I fool myself and my addiction reigns supreme. Only when I have reached the bottom and discovered that I am *fundamentally, absolutely unable*, only when I know with both heart and mind that I am powerless, only then can rescue begin. I must accept the curse of the Beast as my curse. **I must embrace the Beast for what he is—me!**

Fighting the Beast can never succeed. I cannot defeat myself! Ignoring the Beast can never remove him. I cannot escape myself! Pleading, bargaining, badgering, promising can never stop the Beast. I am the Beast no matter what I do to defend or deny it! There is only one thing that I can do with the Beast that is me. I can **surrender** him to God. When I embrace myself as the Beast, all my efforts to control the Beast that was not me can come to an end. My only freedom lies in embracing my broken and desperate self because this bestial curse brings me to the end of myself—and to the beginning of me.

NOT

The am I was not
Kept after me
A grip as firm as the death
I would be.
The am I would be
Was not enough
To keep me from the I am
That was me.
Not me was what I was
And when I was not me
Not was not enough for me to be.

I became not me
Not this or that that I could be

Afraid of being not not me
Afraid to see the is not me
But not me did not make me me.

Who can I be?
Not me and not me
I must have more than be or not to be.
But no one answered
"Just be me."

CHAPTER FOUR

Out of Control

Trust in the Lord with all your heart, and do not lean on your own understanding. In all your ways acknowledge Him and He will make your paths straight. Proverbs 3:5-6

Any battle with the Beast will have to come from power beyond us for the simple reason that we **are** the creature we wish to conquer. Even though it sometimes feels as if this creature is an alien, it is not as though something external to ourselves is attacking us and we simply lack the weapons to do battle. If that were the case, we would only need to find the right tools to do battle. The Beast has aligned our own will against our need for recovery and freedom. Pogo got it right: "We have found the enemy and he is us." However, the freedom we seek cannot be a freedom to simply *overcome* the Beast. That would do nothing more than attempt to tie down the ferocious creature within. We would continue to be shackled to ourselves; in union with the restrained Beast. If we are to have any lasting freedom at all, it must be a freedom that enables us to become something other than what we are now.

For this reason, the biblical concept of freedom is found within the framework of the word "redemption." Our humanness must be rescued, redeemed and restored. We need to be bought out of slavery to the promises of the Beast, in order to become human. The biblical record proclaims that God's unwavering covenant promise of a new order operates on grace, not power. This promise stands in stark contrast to bestial operating principles. When we are in the throes of personal power struggles, we are inwardly focused. We try either to fulfill the promises of the Beast or to control the manifestations of the Beast. Neither is possible. This inward focus removes the hope of God's promise. Obsession with the self-in-control only obscures truly human participation in the grand redesign of the universe.

God's way is very different than the logic of control. God's way is the way of repentance, but repentance presupposes a self that has already acknowledged that it is **out of control** and **incapable of self-repair**. For the repentant believer, control is no longer the issue. Self-in-control must be set aside when the crushing reality of "already **dead** in my present condition" takes hold. No one who is dead has control of anything. The grave sees to it that force-of-will is a moot point. The first step in repentance is acknowledging that I have had it, that I am truly one of the living dead, that I am powerless.

Even if we admit our helplessness, even if we want to resist our addictions, we are not automatically removed from the past effects of pattern engineering gone astray. Gerald May is most helpful in understanding why bestial patterns are so difficult to overcome.

> As soon as one tries to control any truly addictive behavior by making autonomous intentional resolutions, one begins to defeat oneself. For the most part, defeat is due to

mixed motivations. One part of the will sincerely wants to be free. Another part wants to continue the addictive behavior. In any true addiction, the second part is stronger, and so the resolutions fail. The fundamental mind trick of addiction is focusing attention on willpower.[6]

Think of this situation like a computer virus. The original program was perfectly suited for its intended results. But the operator, believing that he could make it work better, faster or easier, added some extra code. This extra code carried with it a lethal virus that has now so contaminated the entire program control center that the only thing left to do is to wipe the disk clean and start over. But that move is so radical, so painful, so disruptive that the system and the operator both resist it with all their might. Since the choice to wipe the disk clean is entirely voluntary, resistance means that the old corrupted program keeps right on going until it finally kills the entire system along with the operator. Even when we know that alignment with the old order is slowly but inevitably choking the very life out of us, we seem unable to voluntarily give it up.

I have often found myself in this dilemma. I know that my addictions to self-in-control are destructive, but (I think) they are all that I've got. What will become of who I am if I have to give up (read "STOP!") the very addictions that are now so much a part of me? They actually form my self-identity. Whenever I try to resist them, I cross swords with

---

[6] Rollo May, *Addiction and Grace*, p.28

myself. Even though I realize that the consequences of my self-in-control patterns are destructive and dysfunctional, I cannot see any alternatives. I have no options because my world is defined by bestial logic. I want to break free, but I don't seem to have the power to act in ways that are different than what I am already doing. What's worse is that when I do try to change my patterned behavior, I feel panic, depression or intense anxiety. I run back to the Beast for comfort. As miserable as I may be afterward, I know that the Beast will take away my pain for the moment. Brené Brown captures my dilemma perfectly: "How can we expect someone to give up a way of seeing and understanding the world that has physically, cognitively or emotionally kept them alive?"[7]

This much I know for sure. Determination alone cannot succeed. I cannot fight myself and win. I have made resolution after resolution. I have experienced shame, embarrassment, public confession, counseling and therapy. But none of these "I-can-handle-it" techniques have ever broken my compulsion to continue the addictive behavior. "Willpower and resolutions come and go, but the addictive process never sleeps."[8]

Our struggles with temptations, attachments and addictions are, in reality, conflicts with spiritual decisions: to remain weak and dependent, to flee self-protection, to embrace pain and suffering and finally to choose to die to the selves we have become. These spiritual decisions are the

_____

7 Brené Brown, *Daring Greatly*, (Avery, 2012), p. 158.

8 May, p. 52.

characteristics of the one person we need to help us. We need the Beast Master.

Five Fingers of the Beast

An example will help us see why confronting addictive behavior is really spiritual warfare. The characteristics of many addictions can be seen in an example of the addiction to sexual attraction. The first quality of any deep addiction is its broad appeal. [9] Certainly sexual addictions exhibit this characteristic. If this were not the case, advertisers would find that the connection between sex and products would fail to increase sales. Just the opposite is true. Sex sells! It sells because all of us are sexual beings and many of us are confused about what that really means. The promise of the Beast corrupts fulfilling sexual identity. In this corruption lies the opportunity for addiction.[10] We have taught ourselves that sexual magnetism is required to be a fulfilled person. We have learned the behaviors of sexual fantasy. We reinforce our engineered pattern with movie star dreams, glamour

---

[9]Any compulsive behavior could qualify, from yelling at employees or family members to the fear of heights. For an enlightening list of possible candidates see May, pp. 38-39.

[10]Using sexual addiction may be an especially uncomfortable illustration for some of us, but there is no question that the addiction is rampant regardless of its hidden nature. Consider the *Janus Report on Sexual Behavior* summarized in *Time* magazine nearly 25 years ago (March 8, 1993, p. 21). It found that 47% of men and 23% of women masturbate weekly, 31% of men and women who considered themselves very religious have had an affair and 71% had pre-marital sex. Patrick Carnes, a recognized expert on sex addiction, has estimated that as many as 12 million Americans suffer from the disease.

magazines, reality television and pornography. This is the second important characteristic. Deep addictions become part of our perceived self-identity. We can't imagine ourselves without the addictive framework. That is not the same as saying that we can't imagine ourselves without the *unwanted consequences* of our addictions. Of course we can do that! We would rather be thin than fat, attractive than ugly, powerful than helpless, rich than poor, even tempered than angry, kind than vengeful. But it doesn't work that way. Because behind all the things we would rather be is the bestial framework of who we are. We are anxious, fearful, proud, lonely, guilty and all those others things that we turn to the Beast to numb. Bestial logic becomes how we think about ourselves.

By the time these "harmless" fantasies begin to alter our self-image, we are so attached to this particular self-image that we can no longer stop the cycles of expectation and discouragement that accompany our experience of reality. In our example, sexual addiction uses and encourages the secret desires we harbor about being sexually attractive and sexually active persons. The addiction reinforces this desire in two ways. It tells us that we deserve to have our desires fulfilled and, at the same time, it chides us that we do not experience these fulfilled desires. This is the third characteristic of addictions. Addictions forge a link between fantasy and reality, but it is always a link of ultimate disappointment. As soon as the addiction draws my inner expectations into the circle with my outer experience, I see that I do not have what I want. I am compelled to either chase the desire or retreat to the numbness of the addiction.

The fourth characteristic of addictions is the power to blur the line between fantasy and reality. Because the addiction offers justification for our desires, we act in ways that we believe will make the world serve our needs. We attempt to control the external world so that it will fit our addictive internal world. We allow ourselves to believe that our external world is out of sync with what we really deserve. We operate on the principle that says, "Do not adjust your mind, there is a fault in reality." But external reality rarely complies with our efforts to force it into molds of our own design. The result is hurt, disappointment and resentment. In sexual addiction, this result produces a litany of corollary addictions: physical image preoccupation, idolization of self-acceptance (love hunger), serial monogamy, pornography, promiscuity, masturbation, etc. We opt for fantasy because reality is too harsh to deal with. Disappointment and resentment set the stage for the fifth characteristic of addiction. Addictions are viciously circular. In our example, our failure to make the world conform to our internal sexual desires produces despair about who we think we are. We feel rejected. We hurt. The addiction tells us that our desires are right and the world is wrong. Therefore, we are left with only two choices: make the world conform through sexual aggression or withdraw from the world into sexual fantasy. We force change in our world by divorcing and re-marrying, having cosmetic surgery, starting an affair. If that does not fulfill the desire, we may become more aggressive. Or we move in the other direction, withdrawing from our mates, digging deeper into private fantasies, and so on. In either case, the addictive pattern is strengthened. We are slowly removed from our own humanness. The addiction is now running our lives. Our freedom has been erased. In our example, we become two different people—one external conforming sexual façade and one intensely private, isolated sexual compulsive. Since we are using addictive behavior to mask other pains or fears, no manifestation of the addiction can ultimately satisfy because the underlying causes remain untreated. But bestial logic does not allow us to draw this conclusion. In bestial logic, we always need more of the same painkiller because the pain won't go away. We can apply the same principles to any other addictive behavior that attempts to soothe our dysfunctional view of reality. Eating when we feel lonely. Drinking in order to dull anxiety. Smoking in order to be accepted. Shopping when we feel powerless. Gambling when we miss the rush of life. Using drugs because we feel worthless. The list is nearly endless. Almost *any* human behavior can become addictive. *Almost*, but not quite, as we will see.

Addictions operate as habitual (instinctual) patterns. We never consciously analyze the way that they work when we are behaving according to addictive logic. We are in overdrive. <u>Intellectual analysis is powerless to break an addictive pattern in progress</u>. This hindsight reflection shows us why addictions are spiritual battles. . Addictions share two assumptions that depend on a deeper spiritual base. The first is that my desires should be fulfilled in my experience of reality. The second is that I deserve relief from my pain when reality does **not** conform to my desires. These critical assumptions depend on one deeper assumption—that the world should be made according to my image of it. In other words, I should be God.

Addictive patterns never call into question my demand for desire fulfillment or my avoidance of pain. The nature of the addiction prevents the reflection necessary to uncover these lies. More importantly, unreflective addictive behavior is purposely blind to its deeper spiritual base because it cannot look upon the truth and continue to operate. ". . . and men loved the darkness rather than the light; for their deeds were evil" (John 3:19). Yeshua said something very important when he called the prince of this world the father of lies. Because the Beast can only live in the atmosphere of lies, he can never allow the truth to be revealed to us. Addictions provide the perfect paradigm for explaining the world. They are viciously circular, interpreting all experience within the paradigm, never allowing any circumstance to seriously unravel the addictive answer.

The Beast Master is capable and willing to break our cycle of destructive addiction. But the logic needed to lead us to freedom cannot be anything like the logic that propelled us into slavery. The logic of the Beast Master is so antithetical to human effort that it shocks us. It seems so backwards, so impossible, that we doubt it could ever work. But it does. It works precisely because it supplants all of the bestial logic that we have adapted to our thinking. It turns the whole world upside down. It begins with a true reality check.

Weakness

The first step in derailing bestial logic is the step of weakness. We must begin where we really are. We are not only weak, we are helpless. This is all that we really have. The Beast owns our strength and uses it against us. Therefore, we must start from utter dependency. Without God, we cannot hope to overcome ourselves. To think otherwise is to be deluded by the Beast.

Even though Yeshua had no dysfunctional addictions to surrender, his actions show that he understood that dependency was the foundation of right standing before God the Father. When Yeshua was baptized by John, he voluntarily took on the role of the repentant servant as a representative of Israel. Yeshua incorporated the step of weakness into every response to the evil one. He knew that the first step in confrontation with temptation is to rely entirely on someone else—the Father Who is the only absolutely unfailing person in the universe. If Yeshua took this position even though he was sinless, how much more are we in need of recognizing our total dependency and following his pattern?

Anyone who has ever tried to combat an addiction knows that the trigger mechanisms are extremely subtle. The engineered pattern has been so well established that it takes only the slightest impulse to set the behavior in motion. Once in motion, stopping an addictive cycle is like trying to derail a forty-ton locomotive moving at high speed. Moses Luzzatto recognized the propulsion power when he exhorted disciples to embrace "watchfulness," the deliberate effort of paying close attention to the smallest details that *begin* a destructive pattern. He knew that if we don't stop the train *before* it moves, we cannot stop it at all.

Addictive pathways are lethal to true humanness. But that does not make them less stimulating or less reinforcing. Their strength lies in the fact that they offer us a world created for our own desires and a way of blocking the pain of disappointment with any other "reality." Their subtlety lies in the addiction's ability to reduce our awareness to instinctual behavior and block our spiritual alarms. Once addictions are learned they enlist us as agents on their behalf. The only way to overcome the automatic patterns of addictions is to just **STOP**.

Unfortunately, most of us have the experience of **wishing** to stop, **hoping** to stop, **trying** to stop and **failing** to stop. That is because we allow the Beast to convince us that we do not need to pay attention to the step of weakness. We listen to the Beast whisper "Power" and our belief in self-sufficiency kills us.

Yeshua's first step tells us to truly abandon ourselves to the strength of another. The only way to stop is to give up starting. Since we are already trained to start at the slightest impetus, we will never be able to stop ourselves. We have worn the groove of letting the Beast protect us so deeply that we are unable to STOP once the track begins to play. We must let someone else furnish the strength to do that.

By now each of us is probably saying, "This all sounds so right, but I have tried and tried, and always I fail. How do I become so dependent that the temptation to begin my addictive behavior ceases to pull me into the same old patterns?"

The answer is found in the second step: Openness is strength.

Openness

Yeshua's second step recognizes that the only protection from the automatic responses of learned addictions is to cease resisting. This seems absolutely absurd. How can we be free of addiction if we do not fight it? Because "cease resisting" does not mean "give in to the impulse." What Yeshua did was avoid the potential of attachment, and the resulting conflict of will, by *deflecting* the temptation rather than *fighting* the temptation. Yeshua never argued with the evil one. He did not present a defense. He did not try to overcome the temptation at all. He deferred the issue to God. Every response was focused not on the stimulus of the temptation but on the person of God.

A fighter learns to close himself to attack. He protects himself by building a shield around him. But when we face addictions, the shields that we build for fighting only serve to keep us locked inside ourselves in mortal combat with the enemy within. Nothing we can do can protect us from ourselves. Building fortresses for protection is only effective when the attack comes from *outside* the walls. Building fortresses to fight addictions only insures that no outside help can get in to rescue us.

Taking the position of the fighter already gives ammunition to the addiction. It acknowledges the strength and power of the inner enemy. The intention is to defeat the person who desires the addiction to continue—but that is *me*! Protecting ourselves can only mean failure. Protecting ourselves is the subterfuge of bestial power.

Our analysis of this second step does not mean that we will find freedom from our addictions without discipline. Discipline is required, but it is not the discipline of the fighter. It is the discipline of the servant. <u>It is the discipline to humble ourselves as weak and failed children before a loving and capable Father.</u> Fighting an addiction can proceed only on the assumption that we are capable of winning. This is the trap of self-sufficiency disguised as the power of resistance. If we think that the secret to resisting temptation and addiction is tied to *our* ability to make ourselves dependent, we have already started on the wrong path. Believing that there is some magical spiritual process that we must appropriate is just as much a part of the attachment to self-sufficiency as believing that we can do it without God at all. The focus of the energy is still on **ME**; the name of the game is still **CONTROL**.

In order to change that perspective and see a real difference, the focus must be on God. That means facing the fact that our addictions are not just disturbing behaviors. They are sins! They are deeply embedded contradictions of our own humanness. Addictions make us less than human. Until we let the hideous truth about our addictive behaviors really sink into our consciousness, we will be playing a mind game; trying to be free of one addiction in order to go on with others. Our real issue is us. We are sinful. Not just because we may have lied, stolen or hurt others. We are sinful because we are committed to our own way. We want to make the world in the image of our desires. We have failed to love from un-self-serving emptiness.

The freedom from addiction that God intends for us is not based on our need to escape from disturbing or disruptive behaviors. It is not based on us at all. It is based on God's purpose to bring us back to true humanness and fellowship with Him.

Yeshua shuns the role of the fighter even in its spiritual dimensions. Instead, he offers us another model—the suffering servant. The humility of the servant comes from a very disturbing fact—we have already lost this battle. No one who stands before God in true recognition of His majesty and our desperation can at the same time entertain a decision to act independently of His will. Allowing temptation to become reality can only occur when we decide that God is not a player *in this moment's drama*. When we realize that our indulgence in addictions destroys our own humanness, we will see sin for what it really is. It is self above all else.

Yeshua shows us how deflection works. He does not take the challenge to fight the battle over temptation. He *submits* to God. His mental energy is turned to God's voice and God's word. He overcomes temptation by capitulating to the Father. He cries to the Father for help and throws himself on his trust that God will provide. He is willing to *wait* for God to answer. He does not entertain the temptation even to resist it. Instead, he focuses his mind on *Who God is*.

When temptations come, they are not turned aside by engaging in confrontation with them. Our built-in responsiveness to the appeal of the temptation has already enlisted our own willpower before we have time to think about it. To fight is to lose. To seek power is to fail. We need the discipline of remembering the real consequences of sin when we face temptations. Sin makes us bestial. That image should drive us to our knees in utter thankfulness that God still loves us. Yeshua deflected temptation by acknowledging that God is not only a player but is the **only** capable player.

As If

How does this help all the rest of us who have already learned self-addictions, who no longer stand at the brink of addictive potential, but are now deeply involved in contaminated core programming? The answer is the same. God's image is stamped into us until we finally erase it in death. We will always have choice. The further we are on the pathway of reinforcing our addictions, the more painful those choices may be. But they are always there.

Yeshua's action is still our model. God cannot be the focus of my mental energy at the same time that I am choosing to reinforce my addictive behaviors. The pathway divides. One direction follows my desire and promises (falsely) pain relief. The other direction moves toward God, true humanness and pain redemption.

God refuses addictions. God refuses lies. To find my own freedom, I must first grasp the intimacy of God's involvement in my struggle. *God is present to me in my addiction.* I may not feel like He is there. After all, the bestial logic closes my awareness to anything but the instinctual pathway of my disease. But my feelings are lying. God is there even in that moment of my most shameful addictive behavior, even when I wish myself to be somehow removed from the actions I am performing. God is there because He says He will be and He does not lie. The addictive attack of the Beast will marshal my own consciousness to convince me that no one could witness what I do and stomach it. But this is not true. God sees it all, knows it all, feels it all. And He still loves me. It is true that God hates my sinful addictive union with the Beast. But so do I. The Beast is bent on taking the good that I am and turning me into evil. And God agrees with my desire for true freedom. In the union that I cannot break, the union that makes me feel the Beast's breath on my neck, God still loves me.

Personally, I need to exercise the "as if" model for myself every day. My addiction begins its cycle of compulsion whenever I feel the emotional pain and spiritual trauma of being abandoned, of not being enough. These are very old triggers for me, reaching back to my childhood. I have turned to the numbing power of the Beast over and over in my life to escape from the experience of loneliness and rejection. But the result has always been the same—more isolation driven by shame. Thicker prison walls. Less light. Today I am learning to surrender these feelings along with my futile attempts to control my Beast. I know that God will never leave me. So I consciously place my trust in Him "as if" He were already providing the nurturing for my emotional well-being that I so desperately need. Surrender is teaching me to wait on God rather than run to the Beast. But this is more than a rational decision. You and I can read all these words and agree with them, but it won't make any real difference until we *feel* them. Our issues are not rational ones. They are *emotional* and it is in the emotional involvement with God that we find relief.

This absolute truth of reality must be understood through surrender. In my addictive state, my will power cannot appropriate God's love to strengthen me. My mental superiority has already been reduced to instinctual mechanism. My self-reliance is shot through with shame and guilt. The inside of my prison walls seep with the stink of my self-defeat. I will never be able to know that God loves me in spite of my bestial union if I wait for a change in my heart before I surrender to His love. I must choose (a very human thing to do) the **"as if"** solution. I must surrender my bestial addiction, my need for control, my failure, my pain *as if* God were entirely ready, capable and willing to repair me. I must choose to give up myself and my reliance on the Beast *as if* God were completely trustworthy to take care of me. What happens next is guaranteed to hurt.

Suffering

Suffering is joy. When it comes to Beast warfare, this is no oxymoron. Relinquishing my addictions causes real pain. May puts it clearly:

> The loss of attachment is the loss of something very real; it is physical. We will resist this loss as long as we possibly can. When withdrawal does happen, it will hurt. And, after it is over, we will mourn. Only then, when we have completed the grieving over our lost attachment, will we breathe the fresh air of freedom with appreciation and gratitude.[11]

> As with other addictions, we do not readily relinquish our attachments to self-images. In fact, we may cling to them more tenaciously than to any other attachments. Although the process of relinquishment is really only a matter of easing the power that certain cell systems have over our sense of self, it can indeed feel like death.[12]

Nothing about the process of confronting God's call to join Him in the wilderness is easy. Living in the wilderness is to be called **out**, away from the power of addiction, away from the pathway of self-protection. It is to live under the judgment of God.

---

[11] May, p. 96.

[12] May, p. 100.

But that is not the end of the story. God has not called us out of ourselves in order to strip us of excitement, wonder and joy. He is not interested in playing the punishing role of policeman, judge or jury. He calls us out of ourselves into the wilderness in order that we might find who we were intended to be. He calls us to His glory! That glory is to know and experience a bonding relationship with our Creator, our Father, our God; a relationship that will make us finally free to choose love unselfishly and become truly human. Spiritual re-engineering begins when we turn ourselves inside out and ask for help in our weakness. It does not end until we know Him, even as we are known.

Too often we fall victim to the religious trap that pain and struggle are the marks of spiritual failure. We have heard too many times that if we only had more faith, if we were only more spiritually disciplined, we would overcome the trials of this life and feel God's eternal blessings. Successful believers, we are told, lead lives of power, victory and significance. Their troubles are over. They have experienced the abundant life and it has filled their bank accounts, their homes and their relationships.

This picture is simply a lie. Living in the wilderness means living in the presence of evil. It means living **through** temptations, not apart from them. It means feeling the pain of sin in our lives, not escaping it. It means walking in the dark night of oppression, not hiding in the light. Yeshua has been there before us. His road was not straight. He had no short cuts. His agonies were real. His suffering meant something. To be a man of sorrows and acquainted with grief means to hurt! But suffering is transformed in the wilderness.

Pain brings awareness. When we touch something hot, the pain of burning our fingers teaches us an immediate lesson. Pain protects us. The next time, we are not so quick to reach for a kettle on the stove. We remember the pain. Addictions numb us to the pain God wants us to remember. <u>Addictions are the leprosy of the soul</u>. They start by removing our spiritual pain sensors. They deaden our internal alarms. Once we no longer feel the pain of remorse, guilt, shame or fear, the addiction can escalate unabated. Pain is there for our benefit. If the Beast is going to rob our inner well-being of spiritual harmony, he must first disconnect our alarm systems. He must be sure that his entry does not set off a call for help. He must replace sensitivity with instinct for self-protection because sensitivity focuses us on God and instinct focuses us on self.

God's reminders of righteousness are planted deep within each of us. It takes a lot of numbing activity to disconnect them. Short of death, they will always be there to push us back to God, to give us a way to cry for help. Spiritual pain increases our sensitivity to the character and will of our Father. It is there to remind us of our dependence and of our failures in order that we might turn to the One who is always ready to receive us. To run from this pain is to run away from the very source of our joy. To numb this pain is to anesthetize our humanness.

Yeshua knew pain. As the only truly human person, he was more finely attuned to the pain sensors in his life than any other human being.

What brought him sorrow and grief shows us just how critical spiritual pain is to our re-engineering. "Yeshua wept." The shortest verse in the Bible found in John 11:35 says something very profound about the Messiah. Death grieved him. This grown man, a man who had seen many people die, who knew the oppression of the Roman Empire on his people, who had ministered to the terminally ill, who experienced the sacrifice of his own cousin, John the Baptist, this grown man cried when he was told that Lazarus had died. He cried even though he already knew that Lazarus would live again.

Yeshua did not cry because Lazarus was dead. He cried because Death had invaded God's creation and held God's children captive to themselves. He cried because the world was so wrong. He cried because we were held in slavery to Death. This is the same man who grieved over the city of Jerusalem (Luke 19:41), who was anguished by the lack of spiritual awareness in his own people (Matt. 12:34; Luke 6:25), who suffered at the scope of human plight (Luke 7:13, and 12:32).

If Yeshua was the first truly human being, then part of that humanness was the full awareness of his environment and the total sensitivity to the passions that it called forth. Yeshua had no addictions to numb his feelings. He had never learned to desensitize himself to the glory of God's creation and the travesty of its corruption. Yeshua felt as we may possibly never feel this side of heaven because he was not fettered by the pattern numbing that we have foisted upon ourselves.

As our addictions take hold of us, we lose our sensitivities. Self-preoccupation turns us away from experiencing the real pain and suffering of others. Self-admiration turns us away from experiencing the challenges and victories of others. Self-sufficiency turns us away from experiencing the dependent interconnectedness of others. <u>We are hindered by our addictions, not simply because they restrict our freedom, but because they remove our human sensors.</u> We are stripped of our abilities to feel – to feel communion, to feel connection, to feel compassion. Addictions allow us to continue in sin because they have numbed us to what it means to be loved by God and to love God.

Yeshua experienced life without filters. As such he was open to the world and to God. He was open to see God's creation and God's purposes as they really are. Yeshua saw things in people that even they could not see because he saw clearly. He did things in this world that we cannot do because he acted consistently with the vision of the new order. It should be no surprise that Yeshua created controversy everywhere that he went. He did not fit, not because he was God disguised in human form, but because he was really human in a world of the living dead.

If we read the Gospel accounts with this perspective in mind, we see Yeshua as the model of true humanness. His submission to God and his faithfulness to the new order act as beacon lights in the world of darkness. They expose us for what we really are. We should experience intense personal nausea over sin. As long as we are enjoying our addictions, or finding relief in them, or avoiding pain through them, we too must fall under God's judgment. Yeshua demonstrated in word and deed just how far from the light our inner diseases really are. But once we face our own helplessness, Yeshua shows us true compassion. He is ready to heal us. He is anxious to call us brothers and sisters. He was sent to bring us back to ourselves.

Dying

Dying is life. Crucifixion is the final part of this process. We cannot experience real humanness until we have died to the false logic and behavior that holds us captive. Gerald May is right when he says that giving up an attachment feels like death. It is death. It is death to the old order. It is death to the things that bind me ever so subtly to themselves. It is death to who I have come to believe that I am. And the Beast does not die easily.

No one can die to the addictions of sin without experiencing the pain of loss, even if the result is ultimately the joy of reestablished fellowship. At the point of crucifixion, each of us must place our addicted self on the cross. The idols that we have fashioned with our minds must be exposed to the light of God's holiness. And in that light, they will have to die.

That means that we will have to die along with them for they are us. We have taught ourselves that we are created in our own image. To be recreated in God's intended image is to put ourselves to death. Unless we die, God's intended image cannot live. Unless we die in the existential process of self-crucifixion, we will surely die in the process of self-addiction.   As a recovering addict said, "I can die with my disease or I can die from my disease." Every forgiven sinner knows the truth of this claim. The Beast is forever.   As addict-sinners, we will never know the extinction of the Beast. This is our sacred curse.   But we can know the death of our compulsions, our out-of-control slavery.   We can know the release from our bondage.   We can know a future undetermined by the hideous past.   We can die, knowing we have surrendered and are forgiven; or we can die crushed by the grip of the Beast.

It is really a matter of choosing one death or the other.   There is no escape from this choice.   To avoid the agony of our own cross now is to flee from the pain that heals.   The nails in our hands and the spear in our side will certainly kill the person that we thought we had to be.   But the other side of the tomb gives us back a person we never thought we could be.   Dying is life.

We need to stop here for a moment and clear up some possible misconceptions.   The first deception is that this is just so much spiritual jargon.   We would certainly be misdirected if the result of this analysis only produced the conclusion that such a program may work for religious people, but it cannot help you and me.   If we did know God, we lost Him along the road of self-destruction.   What we think we need is a cure, not a confessional.

Let us be clear: this is not a "program" at all.   It absolutely is about you and me, not about Mother Teresa or Saint Francis.   The fact is that Mother Teresa and Saint Francis probably already learned what we are trying to feebly grasp.   This message is a message for ordinary people because it is a message of hope for the hurting.

Somewhere along the line we have discovered that life has not given us the real, deep acceptance and affirmation that we crave. Somehow life has not provided the unconditional love that we must have to be truly ourselves. Somewhere we missed out on the fulfillment of our deepest longings for truth and value. We were abandoned. That pain must be either numbed or healed. This message is for us because we are the ones who cry.

The fundamental conviction of every point in this approach is that this deep-seated malaise is, at the very bottom, **only** a spiritual issue. No other approach to our inner dread and disease can ultimately offer us real hope. Certainly, we can dull the pain, but aspirin cannot cure cancer. We may need to treat symptoms, examine behaviors, change patterns, surrender triggers. But if we avoid the pain of our own existence, we fail to be really free of the self-images that make us sick. If there were ever a spiritual need, this is it!

Perhaps the reasons that we are so uncomfortable with an approach that is overtly spiritual, are two-fold. First, to say that the problems we face in the roots of our existence are really spiritual is to admit that we are on unfamiliar ground when it comes to doing anything about them. We would be much more comfortable dealing with a clear, task-oriented approach. Do this, get that. Take these pills. Put more effort into jogging. Change your diet. Get a face lift. These are things that we can **do**. But what do I do when the root problem is in the spirit realm?

And worse still, what do I do when **doing** is part of the problem?

Secondly, this spiritual malaise is finally about sin. And sin makes us very uncomfortable. It means looking at ourselves with total honesty in a framework provided not by us, but by God. Most of our addictive escapes to the Beast are intentional efforts to *avoid* this picture. Even on the surface, that picture is not very pretty. <u>All of our doing cannot cover up what we are being.</u> Our disease is directly tied to what we are, not just what we do. The bottom line is that we are broken, a mess, repulsive to ourselves and to anyone who happens to find out the truth about us. We don't like what we see. It hurts. We need to ask forgiveness of others. We need to reveal deep fears. We need to open something we have kept hidden. So, of course, we are not anxious to expose what we see to the light of God's day, even if it is on a personal cross. To look at what we really are carries fearful consequences. It most certainly carries pain. And it is very hard to believe that pain is the direction of recovery.

On top of all of that, most of us are stuck with the bestial logic picture of God. We know we deserve punishment for our failures of will, for the wrong that we have become. And the Beast is quick to remind us that if we were God we certainly would not hesitate to extract punishment for those sins. We see God as the Great Tyrant of the Universe, meting out retribution for evil. If He exists at all, He scares us. We can barely handle life as it is. We have no desire to add one ounce more to the burden we bear. We push God out of the healing equation because we are afraid of Him.

But we are still sick. That is the thing that just won't go away. All the other cover-ups have not cured our illness. The temporary anesthetic wears off faster and faster. The disease progresses. We know better than anyone how sick we really are. Our own inner being confirms it. This is a spiritual problem! The terror of this realization is that we don't have any idea how to initiate spiritual solutions. Prayers bounce off lead ceilings. Vows are broken. Self-flagellation just leaves us infected. Church services seem to be conducted in alien worlds. Reading the Bible or devotional literature is like pouring water through a sieve. Nothing we do seems to help remove that impenetrable wall between us and God. No wonder we shudder at the thought that we need spiritual help.

The second trap we may encounter is thinking that this approach calls us to a more disciplined path. Once again, we are misdirected. Certainly, examining who Yeshua was as truly human, who God is as truly loving and what that means for you and me, is serious business. But none of this is about resolving to do more, be better, try harder or any other self-initiated, humanly contrived effort. We cannot fix ourselves. In fact, the more that we try, the worse it gets. Self-discipline, even in its most religious form, is not the answer. It isn't even the right direction. We don't need more will power. We need a new will.

Attachment and addiction enlist our own will in the effort to keep our sinful activities alive and multiplying. Our willpower cannot rescue us. We have taught it to numb the spiritual alarms. Now it is doing its job, marshaling all of our own resources to keep the addiction in place. Doing more of anything will not help. Only God can repair this mess. And His repair process calls for steps that seem entirely backwards. As May says:

> Although some new facts and representations may help us along the way… the essential process is one of transformation, not education. It is, if anything, an unlearning process in which our old ways are cleansed, liberated and redeemed.[13]

Finally, we may resist because we find that surrendering leads us toward a frightening emptiness. **This is perhaps the most important truth that we can discover.** It is also the most difficult to understand. This emptiness is not the horror of the inner dread that comes from feeling the anxiety of being somehow lost to our own true identity. The *angst* that we feel when we experience the emptiness of being worthless and alone is the fundamental dysfunctional horror that drives us to the Beast. We avoid its impact by filling our lives with preoccupations and distractions. We cover the pain by pushing it away from consciousness. But it is still there, reminding us that we live without hope, eternally broken, like burial plots with flowers.

---

[13] May, p. 105.

The frightening emptiness that emerges with surrender is much deeper than even our struggles for identity. It is an emptiness bordering the divine. In order to understand how such an experience is central to healing the wounds of being, we must step forward *by faith* because our bestial eyes can see nothing beyond the grave and it is beyond the grave that we must go.

> *More than that, I count all things to be loss in view of the surpassing value of knowing Christ Yeshua my Lord, for whom I have suffered the loss of all this, and count them but rubbish in order that I may gain Christ, and may be found in Him, not having a righteousness of my own derived from the Law, but that which is through faith in Christ, the righteousness which comes from God on the basis of faith, that I may know Him, and the power of His resurrection and the fellowship of His sufferings, being conformed to His death, in order that I may attain to the resurrection from among the dead. (Phil. 3:8-11)*

CHAPTER FIVE
The Empty Core

The kind of emptiness that we encounter in this last step is not *angst*. It is much more like suddenly coming upon an opening in the thick forest, an opening that reveals the entire expanse of the vast mountain range we have been traveling. All the time that we were immersed in the trek, we were really a minuscule part of an unlimited horizon. But we have been so preoccupied with the roots and rocks in the trail that we never noticed the open sky far above the trees, or the almost physical pressure of the space surrounding this great mountain range.

Now, without warning, we turn a corner in the trail and stand on the edge of a great cliff. The view goes on and on into the distance. Snow-capped peak after snow-capped peak, valley upon valley. And all surrounded by space—a vast emptiness. It is this awe-fullness that takes our breath away. It is terrifying because it is so free of parameters. There are no boundaries, no conditions, no concealment. It is open beyond our comprehension. It is frightening and wonderful at the same time. To see the boundaries of our world fall away into openness, to know no limits to what is – this sensory assault can make us dizzy while we stand at the very edge of that great precipice. Life without borders. An encounter with the Open.

Almost magnetically, the Open pulls us toward the freedom of its emptiness. We are compelled to step over the edge, to free fall in its glory. But the danger breaks our reverie. We jump back, not because the vista is repulsive but precisely because it is so attractive. We might actually take the step from the edge. It calls us to let our lives release themselves from the shackles we have placed upon ourselves, and step forward into the unknown emptiness.

None of us know what to do when our carefully constructed boundaries are suddenly torn away. More importantly, we don't even know who we are when we have no walls to give us protection from the Open. The experience of dying to the self is terrifying and, at the same time, compelling in its offer of liberation, for it promises to free us from the constraints that we know have kept us bound to our own form of life. At the same time, it offers absolutely none of the comfort we have come to rely upon to define ourselves. It calls for only one thing: abandonment found in surrender and faith. The wellsprings of our lives gush suddenly in recognition of an essential identity each of us has with this Freedom with a capital F. But it is also Fear with a capital F, because there are no experiences within the boundaries of our lives that provide any formulas or guidelines for who we will be in the Open.

This is very difficult to capture in words. It defies categorization and definition. But there is something here that we must explore. In this exploration, we will find that our language will have to be much less precise, that we will have to depend on metaphors and models to grope our way toward this clearing space. The problem is not that it isn't real. The problem is that this is the ground of our reality. We cannot define It because in a real sense, it defines us. How can we characterize this openness? By borrowing from analyses outside of theology, we can learn some of the critical elements about our experience of this openness. This will help us grasp a little more clearly what it means to die to self.

The Essence of Emptiness

The first thing that we must notice is that our experience of this unboundedness occurs to our consciousness only after our typical parameters have been broken apart. There is no hope of the clearing experience *finding* us, as long as we continue to allow the addictions of our lives to clutter our conscious apprehension. As long as we are subject to the boundaries of self, defined by our attachments and addictions, we are immersed in the behaviors that seek to continue those addictions. This is a state of preoccupation and distraction. As such, it is not open to unboundedness. In fact, the express purpose of preoccupation and distraction is to flee from the sense of expanse and the destruction of boundaries. The addicted, bestial self has no conception of self-identity beyond or outside of the boundaries that it erects for itself. Addictions require parameters. Bestial logic entails the instinctual patterns of limited thinking.

Unboundedness threatens every addiction because it refuses to provide any object for attachment. It cannot become a part of the addictive process. Therefore, the person who knows only the project of constructing boundaries to define self-identity will not and cannot face the expanse of unboundedness. The Beast flees Openness precisely because Openness cannot be subsumed into instinct. Openness is completely free of addictive attachment. It is the expanse of creation where all is possible, including the possibility of becoming who we were designed to be.

The pathway that allows unboundedness to approach us leads us away from attachment and toward self-awareness. We have discovered that addictions suppress our sensibilities. In particular, they remove us from the cleansing force of pain. It is only as we withdraw from the cacophony of non-reflective actions that we begin to see the approaching clearing. Pain and crisis drive us in this direction, against our subjugated will.

Left to our own devices we would most likely never arrive at Openness. Our own will is subservient to the powers of our addictions. It no longer seeks the self that we were intended to become, but rather actively supports the "image self" that we have learned to become. Pain – physical, mental and emotional – breaks the subjugation of the will to the power of the Beast. Pain allows us to withdraw from our addictions precisely because, at the point of pain, the addiction has *failed in its primary task* – to numb us to our own sense of emptiness. Pain breaks through to the self we were meant to be because it breaks the image of the self we have become.

If we have at last learned to be open to our pain, we will go on to discover that beneath the crisis event that caused a break in the addictive pattern is a deeper sense of agony. This is the pain of self-loss. It is not the loss of anything (person, object, behavior). It is rather the sense of loss that comes from feeling the emptiness of who we are. It is the recognition of three elements: that we are not what we are supposed to be, that we do not know how to be what we are supposed to be and that, worst of all, we do not know what we are supposed to be.

In religious circles, this sense of discomposure is often interpreted as a mark of sin. The message seems to be that we are not what we are supposed to be because we are guilty sinners, and what is required is more repentance, more contrition and more restitution. Nothing could be further from the truth. By the time we reach the cliff of Openness, deliberately concealed sin is no longer the problem. We **know** beyond a shadow of a doubt that we are guilty. It is our recognition of sin in the midst of our pain that guides us toward spiritual solutions, rather than alternate addictions, denial or deceit.

The loss that we feel here is at the core of our **original** engineering. In the midst of the corrupted machine resides the remembrance of the original design. Once we come into contact with that remembrance, we touch our true humanity. Suddenly we also know that we are somehow misaligned in our entire approach to existence. We don't fit. We are not at home in the world. There is something very, very wrong. We realize that the piece that is missing is **EMPTY**. This does not mean that there is a space in our lives that needs filling. It is rather that we have been filling a space in our lives that needs emptying. **EMPTY** is what is missing.

The magnetic attraction to step from the edge of the cliff into the Open comes from the identification we feel with the designer. We were made to have a living, fulfilling, joyous relationship with the original Designer. Our core engineering has emptiness at its very center because emptiness is the critical element of the design.

Our project of defining ourselves through attachment and addiction is diametrically opposed to the emptiness we were designed to be. Emptiness cannot be an object of attachment. Attachment presupposes an object presented for possession and a subject willing to engage in the act of possessing. The act of attachment makes the object a part of the self by immersing the object into non-reflective being. Emptiness cannot be immersed into self. Quite literally, there is *nothing* there to be attached. When we truly face God-designed emptiness, we do not possess it. It owns us.

When we stand on the edge of the cliff and peer out across the mountain tops, we lose ourselves. Our inner intended design is remembered. We recognize that we belong to something Other than ourselves. We do not possess the expanse before us. It is not dependent on us. Quite the opposite is true. We are overcome with awe. The mystery of what is invades our consciousness. We are absorbed by the expanse. It takes us into itself with barely a ripple. And yet, at the same time, it is there for us. This is Heschel's concept of the basic structure of human existence: "It is amazement, not understanding; awe, not reasoning; a challenge, a sweep of emotion, the tide of the spirit, a claim on our wills by the living will of God."[14]

Describing this encounter experience in terms of an encounter with unboundedness is only a metaphor. It is a simple mental picture designed to help us understand what the biblical message of dying to self is really all about. It is a frustrated cognitive attempt to speak something that can only be felt. This is an *emotional encounter*, not a rational one. Let us now trace our way back to the edge of that cliff and look at the encounter from the biblical perspective.

---

[14] Abraham Heschel, *Man's Quest for God: Studies in Prayer and Symbolism* (Aurora Press, 1996), p. 30.

Empty to God

When we are convicted of sin through the activity of the Spirit, we are faced with two alternatives. The first is to make futile attempts to numb the pain of that conviction by fleeing to the temporary protections of the medications associated with our addictions. The second is to experience the pain of healing.

Until the crisis of sin in the core of our being becomes a conscious part of our daily experience, retreat into the comfort zone of addictive painkillers will be our automatic choice. Running from God's attempt to break through to us is not surprising. In our self-made image worlds, we have one overriding concern – to protect ourselves from pain. As we have seen, the basis for every form of alignment with the Beast is to control our world so that we can avoid pain. We are the great pretenders, for try as we may, avoiding pain will never make it go away.

Temptations are quite literally appeals to avoid pain. In some cases, the avoidance impetus is obvious. When I feel depressed because life is not giving me what I want, I can be tempted to relieve my depression by turning to alcohol, sex, shopping, eating or drugs. The reality that life does not provide what I want is real. The pain is real. The temptation to take charge of my situation and create my own relief is real. But the problem began with my internal insistence that I should get what I want. My motivation to accept the temptation comes from my frustration of not getting what I want. If I cannot have the world do my bidding, I can at least alter the circumstances to make me feel better in the midst of my disappointment. When reality fails to meet my expectations, I can decide to build another reality after my own image. This is the lair of the Beast.

Every temptation is a temptation to be self-sufficient. In biblical terms, every temptation is an appeal to pretend that we are independent. Ultimately, this logic drives us to see that every temptation is an appeal to be our own god, to make the world after our own imagination. We also find that real pain and real disappointment are the entry points for temptation. Pain and disappointment surround us. We have ample opportunity to choose to recreate our worlds in our own (much more pleasant) way. In some sense, this is critical to what it means to be human. We are really born into a world of troubles, and unless we do something about changing the world, we will be overcome by its intractable lack of care. At this level, pain is good. It brings about the motivation to change things. It propels me to act. In Jewish thought, this is the function of the *yetzer ha'ra*, not precisely an inclination to evil but rather a propensity to alter my present circumstances so that they satisfy me. The problem is that the *yetzer ha'ra* subtly changes my desires into my needs and I begin justifying changes that are entirely focused on what I want from the world, not simply how I can live in God's world. At this point, pain involves active choice about whose world I occupy. Now I must choose whom I will serve.

We have seen that once we elect to cover up this pain with our own created images, we allow our own wills to be co-opted by the need for pain relief. God's method of dealing with sin is just the opposite of pain relief. God asks us to experience the pain that heals.

God cannot cleanse us when we avoid pain. That may sound strange, because God is also concerned about even a sparrow that should fall to the ground in suffering. But we have stacked layer upon layer of self-protection between us and God's call to dependence. The walls of our self-made prisons are thick with bricks of addiction. Only pain can cut through this counterfeit shielding. As long as we are determined to avoid the real disappointments in our lives, we will live outside the healing power of God's good news.

More importantly, we have also seen that we cannot be truly human, we cannot be what the original design calls for us to be, until we voluntarily choose to be **dependent**. This is a sovereignty issue. The experience of God's openness to life does not force itself upon us. We can spend all our lives concentrating on the roots and rocks in the trail, even if those roots and rocks are well established religious habits like attending church, tithing and charitable service. But life does not come from attending church, giving money or doing good deeds. **Life comes from DEATH!** <u>Life comes from choosing to die now rather than letting our physical deaths choose the condition of our spiritual existence later.</u> Therefore, as long as we continue to choose to foster our own self-sufficiency by reinforcing our addictions and relieving our own disappointments by recreating our own images, we will never taste life. All the efforts we put into maintaining our self-images are on the DEATH side of the equation, no matter how noble and moral those efforts seem to be.

We now know that there is no freedom on the side of death. Pain relief is not a cure for the disease. Pretending will not make our lives joyful. Only suffering through the pain of who we have become can lead us to joy, and even that may take a lifetime to complete.

To die to self is to deliberately throw ourselves on God. It can be no other way. To die to self means to sacrifice **all** our self-sufficiency and **all** our self-protection. Anything less is idolatry because anything less will continue the reinforcement of attachment and addiction. Anything less is really me taking care of me.

When we give up who we have made of ourselves, we must trust our identity to someone else. We are no longer the makers of who we are. We are utterly dependent on God to care for us and protect us. He promises to do just that, but in His way and time. Dying to self entails accepting the process and framework that God will provide for our unique identities. And that is precisely why the Beast in each of us squeals and shrieks at the prospect of dying to self. Our lives are no longer in our control (were they ever?). God's unfathomable Openness and impenetrable creativity now have full play with the self we will be. Life without boundaries. The scary and the sublime rolled into one.

Encountering the Openness of God is tasting real life. When we are shocked out of our face-to-the-ground existence, we find the sunshine of grace. God forgives. The power in those two words is indescribable. God knows us. He is not fooled by our manufactured images. He sees what we have become. But He also sees what we were intended to be. And He forgives. He forgives us for what we are. No one on earth, no one we will ever meet, no one we can ever imagine, except the God who made us, can do that. We took wonder and turned it into garbage and still He forgives.

To live in the wilderness is to live under the judgment of God. It is to be as aware as possible that we have made a travesty of God's gift of life to us. We have deliberately and consistently turned the life of Openness into a life of self-protection. But there is another side to living in the wilderness. For if we are conscious of God's judgment, we also know His forgiveness. From judgment comes hope. And with hope comes Truth.

Lest we are seduced into believing this is only a rational, volitional maneuver, we must keep in mind that what is at stake here is our *emotional selves*. Unless we *feel* what God is doing, it will be no more effective than reading a book about playing tennis instead of getting on the court and hitting the ball.

Alethia

The Greek word for truth is *alethia*. It is really a conjunction of two words, the negative *a* for "not" and *letho* which means "to forget." *Alethia* literally means, "not to forget." Its essential character is the unhidden or unconcealed. In this sense, it is an *event*, not a propositional statement. While statements may be true or false, *alethia* says something about an encounter – an event that discloses, that unveils something otherwise forgotten.

If hope leads us to the truth, then it leads us to disclosure. There are numbers of very significant concepts that can be drawn from this understanding of truth. All of them are found in Yeshua's statement in John 14:6, "I am the way, the truth and the life." From a biblical perspective, believing is not based on a set of factually correct statements. It is not true in the sense that the doctrines that describe beliefs are correct rather than incorrect. Believing is based on **the disclosure of God in the life of Yeshua**. Believing is a *lived experience*.

When Yeshua said, "I am the truth," he was saying something far more than simply that he spoke true statements. He was saying that God was being disclosed in him. God was being unhidden. Yeshua is the truth in that he is the encounter event between the unconcealed God and the forgetful children. Yeshua is God's reminder that God has not forgotten us. God is now unhidden. We have forgotten Him by turning from the unbounded Openness to our self-created boundaries. We have covered up the mystery of Openness by placing counterfeit pain-relieving restrictions in our lives and our worlds. We have decided to live in untruth and false freedom.

Untruth is not error. Untruth is the result of each one of us taking on the project of our own self-identity, a project that consists of defining the boundaries of our own life, for us and for God. When we live in untruth, we see ourselves as the ground of our own existence. Therefore, we define ourselves in terms of self-sufficiency (what we can control). We abandon the mystery of dependence on the 'unhiddenness' of God and spend our lives in the incessant activity of organizing and controlling our world or disciplining ourselves to assure our position in the world. To accomplish this task of organizing and controlling, we must constantly suppress the remembrance of Openness simply because it calls into question the entire purpose of our self-sufficient behaviors. *We must forget the mystery of our being.*

The drive to control ultimately spawns crises that lead to the realization of our impotence. This is a realization of our dependence and at the same time, a confrontation with the deeper mystery of Openness. Our forgetfulness pushes us toward pain relief in attachments and addictions. Our failure to control reality brings us the pain of impotence. But our original engineering design beckons us to remember.

The statement of Yeshua shows us that truth is the *encounter* with an unconcealed God. The essence of truth is revelation. Truth does not seek knowledge. *It seeks hope!* In our quest for spiritual re-engineering, we now realize that hope depends entirely on grace. Yeshua's statement that he is the truth tells us that truth is very personal. That does not mean that it is arbitrary, that it is whatever I personally happen to believe. What it means is that the truth of our humanness is to be found, not in systems of thought, rules of conduct or structures of dogma, but in the one-to-one intimately personal encounter with the person who represents the unconcealed disclosure of God.

Yeshua shows us that the emptiness in us is to be considered a great *gain*. It is the mark of God's image. When we embrace the emptiness that we find in us, we discover something absolutely critical about life—our emptiness is the remembrance of the original design—the spiritual nature of being human. The emptiness in us is the clearing space where we encounter the freedom to choose to be obligated to God. The personal encounter with truth that Yeshua embodies means we are free to define ourselves in a way that no other beings in the universe are capable. From the midst of our emptiness, we can choose to obligate ourselves to the encounter with truth and, in the same choice, confront the grace of God. We can **do** the truth, rather than say the truth because the truth is entirely personal. Truth is living fellowship with the living God.

The image that we need to keep in mind is the empty space that surrounds all the things we see in the vista from the top of our imaginary cliff. The majesty of that emptiness is revealed in the fact that it provides the background (the clearing) for us to encounter everything that is unconcealed within that emptiness. It is because of the emptiness that we can experience the unconcealed nature of anything at all. The rabbis speak of this as "white fire," the background of the Torah that makes possible distinguishing all the letters of God's instruction. Without "white fire" Torah is not possible. Without emptiness God is not revealed.

Standing on the edge of the cliff is frightening. We do not do well surrounded by unboundedness. And so we often choose to turn away. That is also a consequence of freedom. We can choose to go back down the trail, away from the clearing, back to the comfort and security of the roots and rocks, back to boundaries.

We turn from the vision of the original design to a design of our own making. We turn from the spiritual creatures that we are toward the bounded creatures that we have chosen to become. We can limit our vision of ourselves to appearances of this present physical existence instead of being projected into the everlasting spiritual existence that God has intended for each of us.

Yeshua's statement tells us that the truth will lead us to grace. In the same statement, he also says that he is the way. There is no other pathway to humanness as it is intended by the Creator except through Yeshua because he and only he is the unconcealed disclosure of God in fully human form. He is the humanity God intended. If we turn back to the roots and rocks of our trail, we not only turn away from God's self-revelation in human form, we also turn away from our own humanness. If we flee from the emptiness inside by attempting to fill that void with attachments and addictions, we deny our own being.

Empty by Design

We were intended to be empty. We were designed to be open. We were created to be the spiritual vessels that only God can fill. There is an awe-full connection between us and our Father and we can only experience it when we stand at the edge of our existence and embrace His emptiness as the essential fact of our being.

To embrace the emptiness of God is to embrace His choice to love us. Nothing more profound could ever be said. The Creator of everything, the Holy Other, the only One worthy of worship—loves us! Here is the final connection. "I am the way, the truth, and the **life**." Life comes through death.

When we remember our intended core engineering, we find that life is discovered in giving. To empty ourselves is to live. Yeshua not only embodied the self-revelation of God, he also embodied the true revelation of humanness. He gave of himself in love. That is the hallmark of God's self-revelation. That is the calling of humanness. To give up what we have tried to hold onto in order to protect ourselves. To die to the effort to fill up the emptiness inside. To *not forget* the emptiness of the Messiah to his God in order to show us what it means to be human.

> The conscience of the world was destroyed by those who were wont to blame others rather than themselves. Let us remember. We revered the instincts but distrusted the prophets. We labored to perfect engines and

let our inner life go to wreck. We ridiculed superstition until we lost the ability to believe. We have helped to extinguish the light our fathers had kindled. We have bartered holiness for convenience, loyalty for success, love for power, wisdom for information, tradition for fashion... There can be no nature without spirit, no world without the Torah, no brotherhood without a father, no humanity without attachment to God.[15]

That Blessed Curse

When did I discover I was falsely made?
The day I first noticed no one knew
That underneath my skin I grew
Some other way

When did I uncover my hopeless agony?
The day I saw me throw away
The ones who wanted me to stay
Forever true

When did I admit I had lost the fight?
The day I first realized
How empty were the open eyes
In my mirror

When did I remember He could heal the sick?
The day I found coffin clothes
Wrapped around my eyes and nose
Inside of me

---

[15] Abraham Heschel, *Moral Grandeur and Spiritual Audacity* (Farrar, Straus and Giroux, 1996), p. 211.

When did I discover my illness made me well?
The day I fell into the tomb
And found it was an empty room
Freed from Hell

CHAPTER SIX

"Behold, the man."

Where can we go to see a living example of the four keys in action: weakness, openness, suffering and dying to self? Where must we search to find a human being who demonstrated emptiness at the core? If we could discover one of us who could show us the way, all of our concerns about surrender might be lessened. We might come to believe.

History has provided us with many role models of humanness. From St. Francis to Gandhi, from Moses to Buddha, we who suffer from the ravages of the Beast are occasionally blessed with a vision of what being truly human means. But to see one who exhibited God's design for humanness perfectly, to see one of us who exercised the four keys of surrender in harmony, there is only one place to look. Two thousand years ago, he was introduced to us with the proclamation, "Behold, the man." Two thousand years later, he is still the true revelation of our own humanity. In the final analysis, there is only one truly human person among us—Yeshua of Nazareth.

His story is a story of conflict. This conflict occurs at many levels. On the human level, it is between the faithful and the faithless, the called and the condemned, the disciples and the deceivers. At the first spiritual level, it is a battle between the chosen one of God and the unwitting allies of the evil one.

At the supernal level, it is a struggle between the Messiah and the demons of this world. Finally, it is a cosmic cataclysm between the righteous but merciful God and a world of god-makers.

While these various levels of conflict rage on every page of the gospels, we are most familiar with the major engagements. We know the stories of the temptations in the wilderness, the trial of Yeshua, the crucifixion and the resurrection. To concentrate our spiritual reflection on these few stories without considering their background means that we will prematurely focus on the level of human antagonists. We will be distracted from seeing that a much greater contest is proceeding in parallel with the human drama. We must turn our attention to this larger conflict if we are to see the true model of the human and the divine.

Imagine trying to learn a new skill. It could be golf, embroidery, gourmet cooking, typing. Anything that you have no facility with today. What would it be like to learn the intricacies of that skill without a teacher? Could you learn to have the perfect golf swing by just thinking about it? Could you make the perfect soufflé from a book? All of us need to see the new skill in action. We want a *demonstration* that we can copy. Otherwise we flounder. That is precisely what God has provided. God sent us a living demonstration of truly surrendered humanness—His son. Yeshua was a man, flesh and blood, in Hebrew, *nephesh*. He had the same emotional options, the same physical needs, the same spiritual desires. In his example, we see what living in emptiness is all about. In his encounter with the evil one in the wilderness, we are able to observe all four keys in action. Weakness, openness, suffering and dying become reality.

Weakness

Yeshua has not eaten for forty days. He is hungry. The evil one approaches him with a completely reasonable suggestion. Why not use his power as God's chosen Messiah to satisfy this basic need? What could be more reasonable than to feed a starving man? How will Yeshua accomplish his mission if he starves to death in the wilderness before he can even begin his ministry?

It is important to notice that Yeshua does **not** answer the reasonableness of this temptation. He turns to God's own voice, recorded in the Torah (Deut. 8:3), as the answer to this seemingly innocuous request. He recognizes the hideous strength behind such a simple desire as hunger. That strength is to be self-sufficient, the author and finisher of his destiny.

The amazing part of this temptation is that Yeshua actually had the authority to do exactly what the evil one suggested. It is one thing to be tempted to perform an act that we believe we can do, but in reality, is beyond our capability. It is quite another to be tempted to do something that we absolutely know we can do. In this sense, Yeshua was actually tempted to act with the full capacity of the Messiah before he demonstrated complete obedience to that calling. He could have done what was suggested, but he recognized the appeal of the Beast.

He had placed his life in the hands of the Father. This meant that he gave his survival into the care of the Father. The temptation to produce food from stones was not a temptation to perform some sort of alchemy. It was the temptation to take control of his own needs, to wrest them back from self-submission to the Father. It was an issue of dependence. Would Yeshua rely on the Father to provide even the simplest things of life like food? Or would he decide that God only needs to be consulted on those matters that lie beyond the realm of usual human domain? Would God be the God of all things, or just the big things?

Our attitude about the basic necessities of life reflects a fundamental spiritual commitment. Do we live under God's grace as totally dependent and forever grateful, or do we relegate God to the parts of our lives that we cannot take care of ourselves? This temptation contained a subtle misdirection about who is really the source of life. It was the temptation for Yeshua as a man to become his own provider: to be like God.

Here is the primordial temptation, no different than the temptation of Adam and the woman. It begins with the suggestion that God has not revealed *all* the truth. "Yes, God says that He will take care of you, but does He really mean it? How do you know that you can trust Him? Just look at what has happened to you in this world." It parallels the serpent's suggestion that God lied when he told Adam and the woman that they would die if they ate the fruit from the tree. God just wanted to prevent them from being like gods themselves. The temptation here is to prove that God's word is true by putting God's promises to the test.

Self-sufficiency is rooted in the lie that God helps those who help themselves. It is rooted in the idea that God favors strength. It is rooted in the practice of impatience. It is rooted in the logic of human achievement. The evil one suggests that Yeshua ask for a personal, private confirmation of God's care by doing a little something for himself according to the power God gave him.

Yeshua recognizes the **weakness** of all human beings when we believe that we can, in our own strength, fight off such temptations. The evil one implied that Yeshua "could handle it on his own," the same implication that derailed the first couple. The potential addiction of self-sufficiency resides deeply in every one of us. To try to fight off this subtle suggestion by taking the battle into our own hands is to play by the same rules of the game we wish to avoid. <u>Yeshua sees that strength comes not from human effort but from human weakness.</u> Yeshua learned obedience through suffering. Here, in this simple example, he learned that hunger was a lesson in obedience. This lesson was not to be undone by succumbing to a temptation to ignore the promise of the One Who was the true source of his sustenance. By refusing an object as common as bread, Yeshua put behind him the potential addiction of self-sufficiency.

Openness

The second temptation places before Yeshua the intricacy of a mind trick. Yeshua has refused the addiction of self-sufficiency by aligning himself with God's care as promised in God's recorded word. The evil one now uses that same authority as an avenue for the second temptation. The evil one quotes from Psalm 91:11 and 12:

> For He will give His angels charge concerning you, *(To guard you in all your ways.)* They will bear you up in their hands, lest you strike your foot against a stone.

It is important to recognize that the phrase in parentheses above is omitted from the quotation by the evil one. This omission changes the truth of God's word into a lie (a half-truth), for it allows an opening that would permit us to place obligations on God for our lack of responsible faith.

In other words, the evil one suggests that God has promised not to allow Yeshua to suffer **no matter what Yeshua might do**. Therefore, the evil one suggests that Yeshua can use this promise to personal advantage by making a public display of divine protection. Such a display would ensure that Yeshua would be accepted as the Messiah since it would offer concrete proof of his divine appointment.

This temptation provides more than just the possibility of absolute proof of Yeshua's status. It also provides the possibility of escaping the suffering that accompanies the task set before Yeshua. It makes travelling the road ahead easy.

Embedded in this temptation is an addiction to recognition, to success and to indulgence. In the words of the tempter, all of these are supposedly justified by God's own word. Why not bypass the agony of the road ahead by putting God's promise to the test now? Why not complete the mission in the most expeditious manner? Why suffer unnecessarily? Why not do it *my* way?

Yeshua sees the dangers, but curiously, he does not combat them with a correction of the misquoted passage. He certainly could have done so, pointing out that the full text (all the rest of Psalm 91 as well as the missing phrase) clearly indicates that those who put their absolute trust in God would be cared for by Him because they were doing His will. God does not promise to preserve every willful action, but only those actions that He first calls us to perform as part of His purposes.

Nevertheless, Yeshua bypasses this argument. Instead he cites a part of Deuteronomy 6:16, "You shall not put the Lord your God to the test, . . ."

Yeshua recognizes that the temptation of the evil one suggested in the misquoted half-truth is a temptation that Yeshua should call the shots, placing himself in position to *force* God to act on his behalf. "If God really will protect you, why not make Him show it? It's for a good cause. After all, didn't you come into this world to display God's glory?"

Yeshua realizes the pointlessness of textual debate with the evil one. He sees that verse-by-verse warfare will involve him in a battle of intellect and will. This is a pathway to defeat, not because Yeshua lacks the intellect and will to combat the evil one with correct exegesis, but because the challenge to enter into personal confrontation with the evil one on his terms also contains the potential addiction of pride. Yeshua is first and foremost committed to life in the Spirit—life totally dependent on God's use of him as a vehicle and channel. Therefore, acting on his own strength and authority, even when it comes to arguing the correctness of God's own word, is not allowing God to fill the emptiness within.

The bottom line is this: Yeshua doesn't take the bait. He refuses to fight. The evil one would like nothing better than to pull us into a similar battle of intellect, even if the context is Scripture. Openness as protection means that we put down the gloves and walk out of the ring. God will do the fighting for us if we are ready to leave the challenge alone. When the Beast suggests a circumlocution for addiction, we must copy the action of the true human. Give up, stay empty and let God handle it.

Suffering

The third temptation bares the real intention of the evil one. Yeshua is given a vision of world-wide power. The suggestion is simple: worship me and I will give you authority over all the earth. This is blatant idolatry. It is no less idolatrous to place self-sufficiency ahead of God (the first temptation) or to manipulate God's goodness for one's own gain (the second temptation), but now the veil of pretense is removed. Now we see what is really at stake—alignment with the powers opposed to God.

The first two temptations implied the same conclusion but they were hidden behind apparently innocuous façades. They were longer roads to destruction because they relied on subtle addictions. No more. The full scope of the conflict is now revealed. The cosmic battlefield has come into view.

What the evil one suggests is that universal acknowledgment of Yeshua's authority can be accomplished an *easier* way. The pathway of the evil one always *appears* to be easier._ But it is built on the false premise that the evil one really has the authority to grant what he claims. The evil one simply states that he, not God, is the ruler of this world and that he, not God, can give authority over this world to whomever he chooses.

Yeshua recognizes both sides of this lie. The truth is that the evil one has power in this world only because God *permits* that power. The evil one himself depends on God's sustaining sanction for his very existence. Therefore, from the perspective of true reality (God's order of existence), the evil one has no final authority at all. The lie in the first part of this temptation is to believe that present control is the same as final power.

The second part of the lie is that the end justifies the means. Yeshua's mission is to establish the final confirmation of God's grace toward Man. It is to overcome death and act as witness to guarantee the coming of the Kingdom. This must be accomplished through the pathway of obedience, suffering and death. The evil one simply implies that a confirmation of the authority of Yeshua,

God's chosen one, can be accomplished without taking God's path, that the final result will therefore justify this change in strategy.

Yeshua recognizes that the call of God is a call to be obedient to God's way. It is first and foremost to acknowledge in thought and action that God is the only One worthy of worship. To suggest any alternative is to circumvent God's purpose. To entertain any alternative is to focus only on the result instead of being obedient to the process. It is more than simple idolatry. Acknowledging any claim to power by the evil one is a subversion of the truth of God's grace flowing from emptiness, suffering and submission, not from control, prestige and authority.

The Beast will do everything in its power to convince us that pain is bad and suffering is to be avoided. Believing what the Beast says about pain and suffering is worse than believing a lie. Believing the Beast is being a complete fool. Every time we run from the pain of God's call to become truly human, we actually destroy a little more of what humanness we have left. We become more like the Beast, a creature of the shadows. Only a fool would run from the very cure needed to save him, but that is exactly what we do. The truth is this: the Beast wants only one thing—for us to die—to die in the most agonizing way possible, by losing ourselves, by becoming other than human. The Beast wants our lives of humanness to be turned into lives of deceit, torment, hatred, guilt and shame. The Beast wants us to hate what we are so much so that we would kill ourselves to be free. And then, of course, he will still win.

Yeshua shows us that the road to humanness, the pathway of emptiness, is the acceptance of suffering, not because suffering is agony but because it is liberty from the Beast. Suffering is God's reminder of our bestial option; a reminder that points us toward the joy of being human. In this temptation, Yeshua embraced suffering as the road of destiny, a road that led him to the right hand of the Father. Suffering is joy!

Dying

There is no fourth temptation in the gospel account. That does not mean that Yeshua cannot give us an example of this fourth key. His whole life is a picture of the key that dying is life. He taught it, lived it and went to the cross to show it.

We can no longer justify, rationalize, excuse or compromise the sin of union with the Beast by claiming that it is an unavoidable empirical fact of humanity. It is no longer possible to simply say that being human means being sinful. Yeshua has come. Yeshua was the true human being as God intended all human beings to be. He has walked among us, talked with us, embraced us, challenged us, lived with us and died for us – all to show us that sin is *abnormal*. All to show us that sin causes an insanity that prevents us from dealing with reality as it truly is. Addiction is progressive because it is part of a battle over ownership. That war will never stop escalating until the evil one converts the image of God into an image of himself. Even the smallest temptations, the ones we are most likely to rationalize as harmless, can carry the frightening prospect of self-destruction.

The excuse that sin is normal is a powerful failure mechanism, prominent in much Christian theology. "Little" sins are so utterly controlling and so absolutely devastating because the progressive nature of **any** addiction threatens the freedom that God has given us. Addiction is sin. It stands between us and God's grace. It makes us dependent on something other than our Father. It prevents us from being ourselves. In the final analysis, sin actually damages **us** as much as it causes God to feel regret and empathy on our behalf. We disappoint God not because He requires obedience by some divine *fiat,* but because we have taken the glorious image that He gave us for our benefit and used it for our own destruction.

For us to live as human beings means that the Beast in us must die. That is the equivalent of dying to self. And since self is all that we know, it means dying to who we believe we are. That seems impossible. Fortunately, there is one who has gone before us. He showed us that weakness is the strength of relying on God. He showed us that openness is the protection of obedience to God. He showed us that suffering is the joy of the pathway to God. And finally, he died to prove to us that life, even life here, only begins when we are empty to God.

We may acknowledge that his life is the true life, but this is intellectual agreement. Now comes the harder part. How do we engage what he has shown us? How do we make intellectual apprehension an emotional reality?

PART TWO

CHAPTER SEVEN

War Zones

How wonderful it would be to find that a new life awaits us just for the asking! How marvelous to be released from the old addictive patterns that suffocate us! At this point, it is not even a matter of saying, "If it were only true." We believe, but like the father who begged healing for his son from Yeshua, we also shout, "Help our unbelief." It's not "if it were only true" but rather, "if it could only be true *for me*." I still need the pain to go away. I still need to look at myself without cringing in shame. I still need to feel and *know* that someone loves me. I still need God as Father.

Yes, I believe that God is able to raise me from the cesspool of my union with the Beast. I acknowledge that He has the power. I even hope that He wants to. But even if He can and does, I am afraid of the consequences. I have never lived without the medication of my secret self. I have never made it through a crisis without the salve of my private sins. I don't know what it would be for me to be without the Beast to protect me. I am afraid to die to myself, not because I like what I am but because I don't know who I would be without my bestial armor.

If I am to live again, I must face fear.

My fear of the unknown me isn't all that prevents me from running to the light. As long as I could maintain the compartmentalization of my secret Beast, I could keep a lid on my guilt. Of course, my ability to hold down the lid on that toxic brew was soon reduced to nothing more than fabrication and denial. But at least not everyone knew. At least I still had some camouflage. Now the light beats at the walls of my prison like heaven's battering rams. The bricks are falling in on me. I am being sunburned with shame from every side. Is it any wonder I want to run to the dark corners of my cell? Is it any wonder that the howl for bestial protection is so strong that my throat bleeds? I have lived so long in the dark that the light hurts me. My skin is scorched, my hair singed. Guilt and shame have attached themselves to me like barnacles to the ship's skin. Wherever they are scraped off, the blood flows freely. I long to be clean, but I shudder to think of the torture of that cleansing.

I will have to face guilt in order to be free.

Finally, I come to the core issue. We have talked about the myth of control. We have talked about the ultimate lie. But now the issues are no longer interesting theological psychology. Now I am on the firing line. All of my days I have spent seeking control. Behind all the façades, I wanted nothing less than to have life my way. I may have tried to keep things going by meticulous management of circumstances and other people. I may have escaped to my personal fantasy world. I may have scoffed at the rules and justified my own interpretations. I may have played the victim role. I may have exercised my self-delusions of being better. I may have opted for narcissistic self-pity. No matter how simple or subtle, no matter what the formal outcome, I was still absolutely, unconditionally committed to me. I just didn't know any other way. I was just looking out for Number One. And now I am realizing that one hundred percent of that commitment is deadly, backwards, toxic, sinful and inhuman. I can't save a little for a rainy day. I can't do a share-and-share-alike routine. I can't keep a secret bank account just for me. I have to give up everything. Everything! My self-aspirations, my self-medications, my pre-fabrications and justifications. My manipulation and gratification. Every endeavor to gain control over my world and myself. All surrendered. It is so scary that the Beast in me bounces from wall to wall like an ape in a cage, creating anxiety and distraction. Defecating on my hope, trying to make the vision of light seem like a phantasm of my imagination. But there, on the side, is God, asking me to trust Him. Asking me to come to Him without reservation, without preconception, without expectation other than to belong to Him.

I will have to face my pride if I am going to live.

These are significant fights. They are literally life and death battles. We will deal with each one of these war zones in some detail. Unless we see that the new order reality has special application to these three battle zones—fear, guilt and pride—we will have a tendency to stay stuck in the old-order principles, even when we want to escape them.

Order in Madness

There is a good reason for dealing with these three war zones in this specific order—fear, guilt and pride. When we want to extricate ourselves from bestial logic, we often find that the first blockade we meet is the war zone of fear. Fear immobilizes us even if we believe in forgiveness. Fear paralyzes our will by focusing our attention on the *loss* that we must face. Fear forgets God's faithfulness. Without overcoming fear, we will be unable to act on the choice to surrender.

As soon as we encounter the faithfulness of God, we are often struck down by our guilt. Guilt leads us to shame and shame destroys our self-worth and freedom. Shame replaces God's evaluation of us with the impenetrability of our own self-determined hideousness. We must deal with this lie if we are to be free to surrender.

When we have accepted God's remedy for guilt, we may be faced with the war zone of pride. Pride resists change on anyone's terms but my own. We will discover that this last war zone is really the command center for all bestial principles. Even though we learn what God has to say about fear and guilt, we will remain a slave to the Beast until we let God do battle with pride.

Together these three war zones present virulent combinations that keep us in the realm of the living dead. We must see exactly how God's kingdom of grace defeats each of these fatal confrontations of the soul if we are to stand the light of God's day without fainting.

With Heart and Mind

We need to say something here about the relationship between heart and mind. Alongside the need for intellectual clarity is the requirement of emotional connection. God is not just a theological construction or a cosmological principle. God is a person. When we contemplate God, there is a great deal to think about, but there is also a great deal to feel. *Swept Away by the Deep Blue Wave of Surrender* ought to be the title of our feelings encountering God. Remember, it is not feelings **about** God, but **with** God.

Thinking believers have a *mind* field to avoid here. Believing is not knowing **about** God; it is **knowing** God! Thinking must cooperate with feeling.

Knowing the facts about spiritual re-engineering won't do us any good until those facts become part of the fabric of our psycho-emotional reality. God's approach to the concept of truth makes personal relationship the critical focus of living. And personal relationships always involve feelings. As novelist Arnold Bennet notes: "There can be no knowledge without emotion. We may be aware of a truth, yet until we have felt its force, it is not ours. To the cognition of the brain must be added the experience of the soul."[16]

---

[16] Arnold Bennett,
https://www.brainyquote.com/quotes/authors/a/arnold_bennett
.html

Examining the lair of the Beast helps us identify the logical and spiritual conclusions of the ways that we have habitually chosen to act. We might think that the next step is to simply abandon whatever combination of inadequate bestial behaviors we happen to be using and choose a neutral ground. Unfortunately, that is not possible. No one can operate in the world without some model for action; some way of interacting with the world as he knows it. It is not possible to abandon our present operating system without adopting a new one.

This is called paradigm shift. We do not move from an inadequate paradigm to some neutral zone where we then pick and choose among many competing paradigms. Whenever we leave one way of operating in the world, we automatically enter another. This is also the reason why we so often move from one addictive pattern of behavior into another addiction, rather than into a world of grace. Smokers know this only too well. It is common to simply substitute overeating for smoking. The addictive pattern continues. It has only changed appearances.

The impossibility of paradigm-neutral positions creates another problem. From the time that we begin to understand the world that we live in, we are busy constructing a map (paradigm) of that world. Each one of us has a slightly different map, but each map has the same purpose – to enable us to live in the world around us.

This map helps us distinguish where we fit in the world. It provides us with ready-at-hand answers to problems we face about relationships, actions and reactions. As we grow, we revise the map according to the input we receive. For most of us, we soon begin to find that the map is more comfortable to live with than the reality that it is supposed to model. The map has stability. Reality is often chaotic. The map is predictable. Reality is disorderly. The map is controllable. Reality is ungovernable, at least by human beings. So the revision process becomes more and more rigid. We begin to **adjust reality to fit our map**.

All of these program restrictions would be fine if it were not for the fact that our maps are constructed around a false reality **from the very beginning**. At this moment, the world is temporally out of alignment with its Creator. It was already broken when we arrived. Consequently, every map constructed to model its existence incorporates the brokenness that already exists in our world.

What this means is that pain, envy, hurt, shame, corruption, deception and many other expressions of brokenness infect each of us while we are still in the map-making process. It is as though we were trying to operate a computer with software that already has a lethal virus in it. No matter what we do to try to compensate for this, our resulting program has bugs. It does not matter if we are accountable for the virus or not. The fact is that it is there. We are left only with the problem of dealing with it.

Therefore, our pathway to true humanness does not require corrections to the cartography of our lives. It requires a map of a different universe. Fortunately for us, God is willing to allow us to incorporate the new universe map into our living. Once the compass points for the new universe are set, our lives begin to take on new headings. The old maps just don't fit any more, even if we attempt to force them to. God is patient. When we keep an old map in the closet and drag it out during times of feeling lost, He will not allow the new reality to be altered to fit the old map. God's world is unaffected by our map-making efforts. Eventually we will come to see that only His map is the correct one. As we go forward into the war zones, we can be assured of this one thing, regardless of how we feel right now: God's map is the map of true reality. The anxiety and fear, the hesitation and resistance that we feel about using this map for our lives is not due to its inadequacy, but rather to its reorientation of who we are. Follow the map. It will take you home.

CHAPTER EIGHT

Fear

. . . yet not what I will, but what Thou wilt. (Mark 14:36)

"I'm afraid."

When a child whispers that short sentence in the middle of the night, something happens in our hearts. No matter how many times we have told them that they must now close their eyes and go to sleep, no matter how many times we have threatened to shut the door or turn out the bathroom light, no matter how tired we were when we dragged ourselves to the bed, the parental desire to protect and comfort comes flooding back to our bodies and minds. We are energized to act. We reach out to touch, to caress, to kiss these precious little hands that so desperately need our assurance. We wipe away the tears from those innocent eyes and squeeze ever so gently this little human person now holding on to us as though we were the only refuge in the world.

"It's all right. I'm right here. I love you."

The words come without beckoning. The rush to emotion separates the evil dark from the restful night. At this moment in time, nothing, absolutely nothing is more important than the emotional and mental security of this small dependent being. Love stands up against fear and compels it to be unmasked.

Gethsemane

Two thousand years ago, a man fell to the earth in the middle of the night. His legs did not collapse under him from bodily fatigue. He was used to walking many miles in rough terrain. His arms and shoulders did not give way from lack of sleep. He often stayed awake until the early morning hours in desolate places. His heart did not feel the race of adrenaline because he was surprised by the circumstances. He had known for many years that the goal of his life was to come to this place. He fell to the ground in agony because he encountered the face of fear.

When Yeshua entered the Garden of Gethsemane, he needed to find the reassurance of his Father. He knew that within a few hours the greatest physical struggle of his life would begin. He knew that he was facing his own death. He did what he had always done. He went to be alone with God, to draw from his spiritual connection the life blood that had kept him going for years of misunderstanding, ridicule, rejection and frustration.

Certainly, there had been victories. He had seen the downtrodden of the world made whole. He experienced the touch of God's hand in miraculous ways. He knew that His Father's kingdom was breaking into the old order. But it was a mixed bag. While he proclaimed the Kingdom, those closest to him always misunderstood it as political power.

While he brought a message of freedom, the contemporary religious teachers questioned his authority and proclamation. While he dedicated himself to the outcasts of the world, his most likely compatriots turned a deaf ear to God's signs. No matter what he did or where he went, there was always controversy. So he often came to the Father for consolation, direction and renewal.

The culmination of his life's work was at hand. Now he needed more than ever to know the security of having His Father's arms wrapped around him. Now he needed more than ever to hear His Father's voice whisper love and care. Now he needed more than ever to have His Father bless him with a compassionate touch.

It's Not Metro Goldwyn

This was not a Hollywood version of the crucifixion preamble. The gospel narratives clearly show that Yeshua understood for some time prior to the cross that he would have to die at the hands of sinners. These same records also show Yeshua resolute before his accusers and executioners. Not only did he show no sign of doubt about his outcome, he also endured the physical pain of scourging, torture and crucifixion without faltering.

We do not need to look far into the story of the death of the Messiah to see that the physical pain inflicted upon him must have been intense. We know that the Romans devised crucifixion precisely because it was the most painfully slow method of killing they could concoct. Yeshua was not subjected to the usual Jewish execution of stoning for his alleged offense of blasphemy. He was put to death in the Roman way, under excruciating circumstances, for the crime of sedition. Yet he did not complain, agonize or collapse. It was not the fear of painful physical death that caused Yeshua turmoil in the garden. It was something else, something far more awful than the coming agony of his crucifixion.

If Yeshua was prepared to face his own death, even a death at the hands of the Roman torture machine, then what could it have been that was so frightening that he literally could not stand when it confronted him? For this answer, we must go back to that moment in the middle of the night when our own children call to us to protect them. We must think about our response, our instantaneous heartfelt compassion, reaching out to this small human person who is an extension of our own being. We must remember parental love, knowing that even though the fears of the child are unfounded, the child still needs our reassuring presence.

Concentrate for just a moment and let this experience overwhelm your senses. Remember what it is like to have that little body cling to yours for safety. Translate this experience to the Garden of Gethsemane on a cold Spring night two thousand years ago.

Yeshua lived his life as an extension of the Father. That does not mean that he wasn't just as human as you or me. What it means is that he was totally alive to the presence of God as the central focus of his very being. He was the only human being who was not a broken image. He understood who he was and who God is in such a way that he was able to maintain his connectivity with his heavenly Father as the fundamental ingredient of his self-identity. In other words, when Yeshua said that knowing him meant knowing the Father, he was at the same time saying that his identity as a human being (his ego, if you will) was so in tune with the Father that they were inseparably linked. In Yeshua's own mind, there was no break between God and himself. While all the rest of us live lives of brokenness, Yeshua had never experienced such a disconnection between God and himself.

Normal Human Being

You and I are anesthetized to the pain of a broken connection between who we are and who God intended us to be. Sin not only separates us from the Father, it also deadens our sensitivity to this separation. It separates us from our true identity. Even though our feelings of separation are numbed, we still reap the consequences of this separation. We suffer, we cry, we hurt, we agonize, we despair.

But we do so on a limited scale. We have never really known what it is like to be one hundred percent in line with God's heavenly touch. When we break through this veil of tears and find that God welcomes us with open arms, we experience tremendous joy. But even that joy is dulled by the battering that we have chosen to give ourselves by maintaining the patterns of separation in the first place.

Yeshua comes to us from the other side of this woeful equation. He moves toward us from the perspective of one who is truly human, who has felt and continues to feel the complete active presence of the Father. All of this inner glorious union was true of Yeshua's daily experience until he came to the Garden. In those moments in the Garden, Yeshua became more like you and me than we could ever imagine. We are so afraid to face the truth that Yeshua faced that we deliberately turn away. But Yeshua could not turn away. This was his hour.

The fear that struck Yeshua to the ground was the fear of experiencing brokenness – fear of separation from the Father. For Yeshua, this was not the result of sinful neglect or willful disobedience. It was not a separation brought about by pride. Yeshua did not live his life in self-sufficiency. He knew that he was totally and absolutely dependent on his Father and that his Father wanted it that way. Consequently, for Yeshua, the man who was truly Man, separation from the Father meant nothing less than the destruction of his very identity. The encounter in the Garden was the ultimate test of dependency because he was about to die trusting that God would act according to His promise *after* he was dead and in the grave.

That night, Yeshua came to the Garden to seek the face of his loving Father. But when he opened his eyes, he looked straight at death, the final defilement of creation and the ultimate end of human existence—unless the Father acted. Yeshua was being asked to commit voluntary psychological identity suicide in order to save people like you and me. He was being asked to give up the very person that he was, the very essence of who he knew himself to be, in order to take on the mantle of a broken humanity. For Yeshua, this meant being fully sentient of all that brokenness means. There were no filters between him and extinction. He had not practiced blunting the shock or agony of being removed from God's presence. He was about to experience the end of who he was, fully conscious that *life* in connection with the Father would be broken by the grave. The only consolation was the promise of resurrection. But that meant absolute trust when there were no cards left to play.

It might have been different if God had asked us to drink that cup of judgment. To our great misfortune, we know what it means to be separated. We know because that is the way we live— separated from God. Even in this loathsome state, God's grace protects us. We rarely live with the true pain of that separation. God is willing to let us see glimpses of our real condition in order that we might realize just how wretched our condition really is. But even then, He provides us with filters that screen the instant paralysis an unprotected visage would bring.

We already live in the dead world. We just don't know it. For us, the ones with dampers and blinders, a step away from the presence of the Father might not seem too terrible – certainly not as terrible as the punishing agony of the cross.

But Yeshua knew better. Yeshua knew the sublime glory of the Father's love. He knew the majesty of the Father's care. He knew the serenity of the Father's concern. He knew the peace of the Father's will. Yeshua knew what being human really was because he was the true child of the Father.

So when Yeshua came to the Garden, he looked from the vantage point of true humanity into the foulness of death. Physical torture meant nothing in this context. Losing his life was an oxymoron of the material world. Yeshua was attuned to the spiritual dimension. In that context, the real battlefield stretched before him. Would he trust the Father to the point of extinction?

Spiritual Paralysis

It is significant that the temptations in the wilderness were not psycho-emotive appeals. The three temptations dealt with issues of power – power over the inanimate world, power over the individual's world and power over the social world. On these three scores, Satan failed to trap Yeshua in behavior motivated by selfish gain. Luke's gospel foreshadows the temptation in the Garden when it says that the devil departed from him "until an opportune time."

After the temptations in the wilderness, Yeshua attacked the power of this world with a vengeance. He restored the Father's conception of wholeness to those who were sick, both in body and in spirit. He threw out the henchmen of the Evil One. He disrupted old-order thinking wherever he found its curse on God's children. Until Yeshua reached the Garden, the gospel stories are real battles of might.

Yeshua removed the film from our eyes and revealed the presence of God's simultaneous dimension. In that dimension, the cosmic battle between God's holiness and the ego of the Evil One rages. Yeshua's invasion brought into focus the true issues of life and death. He showed us that the world revealed by our five senses is not the whole picture. What we saw through him was a glimpse into the much bigger "spiritual" world.

That does not mean that our world doesn't count. In fact, Yeshua's activity right here in our midst says just the opposite – that the events of this world count more than we ever could have imagined. Consequently, what happens here, what we choose or do not choose to do, is much more auspicious than we could have ever imagined.

The power struggle was over when Yeshua reached the Garden. God's man had defeated the enemy stronghold from within. The kingdom of this world was finished. It was only a matter of time.

But when Yeshua came to the Garden in the middle of that night, the Devil found his opportune time. He whispered into Yeshua's ear with that thin, scratchy voice that runs chills down the spine. He murmured one single word: *separation*. It was enough to bring Yeshua to the ground. For a man who acknowledged only one identity, only one Lord, only one Father, only one self, this single word was the entrance to the unthinkable. The child cried out in the night and was answered by the specter of disconnection.

In Dante's description of hell, the tenth level, the worst position, consists of solid ice. Human beings who sink to this level are frozen forever in isolation with themselves. We can only begin to imagine what it would be like to be completely separated from others. In our own history, actual cases of this sort of separation have led to insanity. But hell is not only separation from other human beings, it is separation from God. It is separation from God's gracefulness – a grace that is responsible for the world of sensory stimulation showering itself upon us. Even when we are alone, we are in the midst of relatedness. We experience the earth and its beauty. We relate to our environment, the give and take of sensations, the complex interconnectedness of our very living. Imagine, if you can, separation from this. Imagine disconnectedness. No bodily sensations. No environmental interactions. No sight. No sound. No anything. And **no escape**, ever!

Yeshua looked into the night and saw the end of Being. It was not physical death that turned his stomach. It was confrontation with true separation. And it was hideous.

You and I live in a form of hell. We are separated from God until we choose to repent. We spend our lives covering up those fearful feelings so that we can cope with the gnawing inside. We do everything and anything to pretend that life depends on us. We hide, we run, we mask, we ignore. If we were with Yeshua in the Garden, we would have fallen asleep just like his companions. We would have never seen what was really happening right in front of us. The film on our spiritual eyes is too thick.

But once in a while, the scratchy voice whispers in our ears. It creeps up to us from behind. It puts a bony finger on the back of our neck and suddenly we know that we are vulnerable. We get a small sample of what it means to be truly alone, separated. Even this tiny dose is enough to make us sick. For we are already broken. Running through every fiber of our being is the consequence of separation. Running through every relationship, every circumstance in this whole panorama of existence is the fear of isolation. In our world, we can **NEVER** be sure of anything. The power of the Evil One still holds sway. As long as this power has one single ounce of fight left, it will go on turning us toward fear.

Fear paralyzes. It is a self-fulfilling condition, for as soon as I become fearful, I can no longer act. And when I cannot act, I perceive myself as afraid. Our present living hell is nothing more than a slightest whiff of a soon-to-be overwhelming odor. It is the stench of abandonment coming to meet each of us from the dark tunnel.

We have good reason to believe this fear. Our hopes of trust in this world have been dashed on the rocks of unfaithfulness. Our wishes for security have been disappointed. Our lives are full of experiences that justify our fears. But most importantly, we have learned not to trust ourselves. We know better than anyone how much we have cheated on trust, broken promises, told white lies, kept quiet when we should have been counted, run when we should have stood the ground. No one has to tell us about the untrustworthiness of this world. We are living examples of the fact. We condition ourselves to be afraid of separation precisely because we expect to separate. Every time we abandon another we reinforce the probability of being abandoned ourselves.

This is why we are so susceptible to the fear of separation. We know that if we were to be absolutely counted on, we might fail. And if we would do it, we reason, so would they. The smell hangs like Sulphur dust in our own air.

Yeshua's nostrils were filled with this stench. He found himself suffocating, his chest tight with pain, his head reeling. Death, real disconnection, had come calling. The real battle of the crucifixion was being fought in the quiet of this garden. Yeshua learned instantly what we have pretended not to know all of our lives. There is something here that wishes to destroy us alive. Something very evil, totally unrepentant, completely hideous. It lies waiting for us.

Yeshua was afraid – so afraid that Luke says an angel was sent to minister to him so that he would not **die** there in the garden. But just at the point of overwhelming fear, Yeshua showed us all why fear is impotent. Fear forgets God!

Yeshua spent years dealing with the attachments that cause human beings to place idols in their psychic environments. He remained faithful to his calling because he learned to be utterly dependent on God the Father. Now the most important event of God's cosmic plan was about to be accomplished. With it came something so hideous that even Yeshua staggered. At this moment, in his greatest vulnerability, the Evil One presented the most subtle temptation that any human being can ever face – to make an idol of the relationship with God. Yeshua was being asked by the Father to give up the very thing that had sustained him. He was being asked to sacrifice the bond of unity with God that had grown so beautifully over the years. He was being asked to be obedient and yield his very identity with the Father – for the sake of those who were about to torture him to death. At this precise moment, the Evil One smiled. He crept up behind the struggling, agonizing man in prayer and whispered in his ear,

"God doesn't really care about *you*. He only wants His own way. If He really cared, He would see that without Him you will be nothing. If He really cared, He would protect you from this. He would love you enough not to want you to be separated from Him. You've done enough. Look at all you've accomplished. Look how obedient you've been. Look how you've already suffered. And now He wants you to let go of Him? How can you do this and still be who you are?"

When Yeshua staggered under the specter of the hideous consequences of separation from the Father, he found his strength in his relationship with the Father. Yeshua knew, just like you and I now know, that God is faithful. Everything and everyone else could, and sometimes does, fail us. But not our heavenly Father. His constancy is written into the very Being that He is. He cannot be other than faithful. When He says that He loves us, He means that He loves us **NO MATTER WHAT**. There is no "if," "but," "unless" or "because" with

God. He loves us, full stop! Our fearfulness is not a reflection of God's attitude toward us. Fear resides on our side of the equation.

Self Inside

Fear is a subtle corollary of bestial logic. The internal structure of fear is still based on the myth of self. In order for fear to perform its magic of spiritual paralysis, it must begin by convincing us that we are different, special. It must delude us into thinking that no one else could have ever felt like this. The power of fear is the power of isolation, to make me believe that I am abandoned. The Beast in us works this logic to perfection. In an instant, every previous rejection is recalled as confirmation that we are totally alone. In the blink of an eye, the Beast pours out our desperate loneliness in order to convince us that the growing sense of being forsaken is the true character of reality. And, of course, it is easy to believe. As desperately as we want to know unconditional love, we also want to have unconditional power. Our sacred curse maintains that constant tension between being a creature, and wanting to be the Creator. Since true reality belies our delusion of possessing Creator power, we have plenty of evidence that we are alone. After all, there is only one God and He is not us. The Beast can use even this theological truth to hammer us with our desperate finitude. The result is fear – the fear of facing the unalterable truth of our utter dependence. The fear of letting go of that myth of control. The fear of not being God.

This is an amazing paradox. We are afraid precisely because we finally see who we really are.

Our deluded self-concern is shattered in the face of the Creator. We are afraid to be dependent creatures, but that is exactly what we must acknowledge if we are ever to surrender our fear. We stand before our Creator whose arms are outstretched in loving embrace and we tremble for fear that He will not care for us. No human being who was not infected with the utter futility of the Beast could ever resist such a demonstration of love. No infant, the most utterly dependent creature in the world, resists the succor of its mother's breast. Yet our fear stands between us and our God – a fear that is illogical, unbelievable and impossible – a fear that could only be based on our own self-failure. A true mark of the Beast.

Help from Outside

Yeshua knew that God, his Father, was faithful *without qualification*. Therefore, Yeshua's response to the fear of separation was re-commitment of his trust in the Father's character. In spite of the fact that this child opened his eyes in the dark and saw the face of Evil staring at him, he **chose** to remember that his Father **always** loved him, even now, even in this moment of fear. He chose to remember that his Father's feet were coming down the hall even though he could not see them. He chose to remember that his Father's words of affection were being spoken even though he could not hear them. He chose to remember that his Father's loving arms were being wrapped around him even though he could not feel them.

And as soon as he chose to trust what he knew to be true of the Father, in spite of the absence of its present verification, the *fear* of separation left him.

That did not mean that the call for separation was annulled. That did not mean that the demon haunting him disappeared. It meant that Yeshua renewed his own mind with the understanding of who God is. It meant that even though the task in front of him would be no less painful, no less demanding, no less difficult, he could face it knowing that his Father was with him.

When we face our small samples of separation fear, we now have someone just like us who knows exactly what we are afraid of. In fact, we now know that not only does Yeshua existentially identify with our fear, he went beyond any degree of intensity that we will ever face. He faced total abandonment from the platform of total harmony. He went from complete connectivity to absolute separation.

We will never have to face that prospect. We will always move from one state of brokenness toward another state of brokenness or, through God's grace, toward true humanity and spiritual childhood. We never need to be alone in our fear again. The *mind* field that whispers in our ears has been forever destroyed, if we will only open our spiritual eyes to see its grave.

Is it wrong to be afraid? Anyone who has ever faced the Beast knows that fear is an ever-present constituent of that unholy union. But being afraid is not wrong. Being afraid is one of *God's silent alarms* put deep within our consciousness to warn of us impending danger and to cause us to focus on His absolute reliability toward us. Being afraid is the built-in reminder of our dependency. Like so many other natural alarms, fear becomes a part of bestial logic only when it disturbs our inner moorings in such a way that we forget God. The temptation to be afraid is an opportunity to surrender our finitude once more to the Creator. The *sin* of fear is to forget Who God is.

For all eternity, this fact has been established. God is faithful. The paradigm case has been given. If God loves us so much that He remains faithful to us even when we stand in the presence of the hell of separation from Him, then we have the answer we seek. When Yeshua said that he had overcome death, he did not mean that he had only put aside physical termination. He meant that the chains of death itself were broken. He meant that you and I have been given freedom from the inner disease that saps our lives. Our Father has thrown out the demon and lifted us from the fearful night of separation.

We fail each other. We fail God. But He will never fail us. The trap of fear is finished. Our Father loves. His son believed him and chose to follow the calling to confront disconnection in death. As a result, you and I have been rescued from ourselves. The time of fear is over.

Since then the children share in flesh and blood, He Himself likewise also partook of the same, that through death He might render powerless him who had the power of death, that is, the devil; and might deliver those who through fear of death were subject to slavery all their lives. (Hebrews 2:14-15)

What is left to say about being afraid? This is left. Celebrate God's faithfulness! Drink in His mercy! Ponder His majesty! How wonderful the Lord Who made us so marvelously! What other creature has the opportunity to turn self-logic on its head and see the blessing in adversity, the discipline in hard choices, the power in weakness? In the end, it is God, only God, Who is faithful when we are not, Who loves when we do not, Who forgives when we do not.

Our fears and temptations are our pathways to the cross, the chance of a lifetime to learn obedience through suffering. To drink the cup of God's judgment with Yeshua. To learn to die to the power that would keep us from being truly human, truly free. The result is to be glorious:

For I consider that the sufferings of this present time are not worthy to be compared with the glory that is to be revealed to us. (Romans 8:18)

Welcome to the morning!

CHAPTER NINE

The Iceman Cometh

Simon, Simon, behold, Satan has demanded permission to sift you like wheat; (Luke 22:31)

We have an accidental encounter in the grocery store with someone we slandered in gossip. As the nausea rushes into us, we find we cannot look into her eyes.

The person we climbed over to get the promotion by taking credit for his work unexpectedly shows up at a business meeting. While we try to focus through the hot flashes of embarrassment, we think of excuses for exiting.

The spouse who was secretly betrayed finds a letter we saved and uncovers the truth. While our legs collapse beneath us, we shout louder and louder denials.

Guilt is an illness of the soul. It produces spiritual nausea. It is sin poisoning and just like its physical counterpart, it throws us into retching convulsions. With our heads in the toilet of life, we find that even when there is nothing left inside, we go right on vomiting up our worthlessness. Guilt is debilitating.

Guilt is also destructive. When we are in the midst of its grip on our lives, we feel the shake in the legs, the flash of heat through the stomach, the blur of vision and the lightheadedness of fainting. We are squeezed in the vice of shame and defeat. We are crushed. Our internal agony knows no relief. We wish to die.

Because the experience of guilt is so awful, we do our very best not to allow it to occupy space in our lives. We are careful to divert its arrival with displaced attention. We prevent its display with meaningless diversions. We avoid its calling with mindless routines. But still it comes.

Gethsemane II

One Spring in the first century a small band of students gathered around their teacher in customary tutorial manner. The teacher posed a question to them, testing their observational abilities and conclusions. Several of the students offered answers drawn from overhearing other conversations.

Then the teacher asked a more direct question. He posed the same topic while seeking the students' personal opinions. A former fisherman had a flash of insight that overshadowed every other answer. Simon proclaimed, "You are the Messiah, the Son of the living God." For that statement, Shimon Petra received the greatest compliment any student could ever have: "Blessed are you, Simon Barjonas, because flesh and blood did not reveal this to you, but My Father who is in heaven." Yeshua renamed Simon to commemorate that event. *Peter* was on a supernatural high. He had been singled out, given great praise and told that the *qehillah*[17] of Yeshua was to be established on the dependability of his proclamation. No one could have felt more elated. In the same week, Peter was selected to accompany Yeshua mountain climbing. When the four men reached the top, Peter, James and John witnessed the confirmation of God's anointing on their leader. Yeshua was transformed by God's glory. Peter saw a direct divine intervention into the ordinary world of mankind. It was so overpowering that he and the others fell on their faces in fear. Peter certainly felt his privileged status as he descended from that mountain top.

Just when he thought everything was going great, the old order principles were preparing for a war zone battle in Peter's life. His elation collapsed in a single night. His life was undone in three short encounters. He was plunged into guilt.

That night started peculiarly. His leader seemed withdrawn at dinner, saying things that hardly made any sense. They had just experienced a tremendous victory. After hiding from the crowds for months, his leader had suddenly decided to go to Jerusalem. This was what all the students had been hoping. Now it became a reality. The crowds were ecstatic. Yeshua demonstrated authority and power over the hypocritical religious rulers. The crowds backed him. Everyone was on edge waiting for the leader's

---

[17] *qehillah* is the Hebrew equivalent of the Greek *ekklesia*, a word that does *not* mean "church," but rather an assembly called for a purpose. Since Yeshua addressed Shimon in Hebrew, he would have used this word, and what it means is not the same as our translation, "church."

announcement of a political *coup*. Everyone could feel the Romans quaking in their boots.

But instead of a victory celebration, Yeshua seemed unreasonably withdrawn. He was unusually contemplative, speaking about blood, conflict and persecution. He seemed preoccupied and oblivious to the excitement. He started talking about this "death wish" idea again. The most unsettling thing was his direct comment to Peter. Yeshua had taken him aside and said that Satan was going to sift him like wheat. That sent a chill right through the man. He had seen enough of demons during his journey with Yeshua to know that he wanted no part of that. But Yeshua added that he prayed that Peter's faith would not fail. Then he said a very curious thing to him: ". . . and you, when once you have turned again, strengthen your brothers." Peter just didn't have a clue. He wrote it off as one of those dark sayings Yeshua was famous for uttering.

Peter affirmed his allegiance and put in a reminder of his leadership at the same time. "Lord, I am ready to go with you to both prison and death." Surely that was safe to say. Their moment of victory was just around the corner. "If we can just get him through this night." thought Peter, "we'll be on a roll by morning." Peter was convinced that neither prison nor death were in the cards. Soon they would be marching in the streets with thousands behind them and God alongside them. Who could stop a leader who could raise the dead?

Then Peter got his pride slapped. Yeshua looked Peter straight in the eye and claimed that he would actually deny him three times in the next few hours.

Peter was embarrassed. Peter was affronted. Peter was hurt. How could Yeshua say such a thing, and in the presence of the others? His status in the group had been challenged by the teacher. He held his tongue, but his heart was angry and broken. He had been around long enough to know that confrontation with Yeshua was a loser's game. He let it pass. He tried to forget. Tried, but failed.

When they got to the Garden, Yeshua was more upset than Peter could ever remember. He saw his leader trembling, agonizing. "Why now, of all times? Just when we are within arm's length of real power. Just when I am about to become someone really important. Perhaps the strain has been a little too much. A night of quiet meditation will put him back on track," thought Peter to himself.

A little of the previous sting of admonition was erased when Yeshua asked Peter and the two others to come with him a short distance away from the group. He heard Yeshua saying something about watching and praying, but his mind was on other things. He found himself in an inner battle of his own.

On the one hand, he knew he could be a great commander in the new regime soon to be a reality. He saw the opportunity of a lifetime. It was just recompense for following this man through three hard years of wandering. It was what he deserved for being so patient with the sort of on-again, off-again politics of the last eighteen months. Now he would finally get the recognition he deserved.

On the other hand, he was disturbed by Yeshua's questioning of his loyalty. He could suffer the embarrassment if things turned out as he expected. But why would Yeshua think for one moment that he wasn't cut out for this job? Peter still remembered that Yeshua himself had said he would build the assembly around Peter's insight. That's where he got his new name. Not Simon, but Peter - the ROCK.

Now, suddenly, Yeshua was addressing him as Simon again. What had he done? It was too hard to figure out. He closed his eyes. Fatigue settled upon him. He slept.

Out of the blankness of sleep, he realized that someone was standing above him. It seemed like just a few seconds had elapsed. There was Yeshua, sweat glistening from his skin in the moonlight. Yeshua's address brought him to consciousness like cold water in the face. "Simon, are you asleep?"

Simon, the old name. The name before he had become the honored one. By the time Peter came to his senses, Yeshua was moving off into the night again. Peter mentally kicked himself for being so remiss. "How can I show him that I am the right man for the job if I can't even stay awake? Well, it won't happen again. Not tonight!" He felt some consolation in the fact that the two others were also asleep and that none of the larger group could see them. At least it was not so embarrassing as the scene at dinner.

His mind still held this thought when suddenly his eyes jerked open. He had done it again. Asleep.

And there was Yeshua, right in front of the three of them, just watching. The blood rushed to his head. He tried to say something but the words would not come. He pretended that he had only closed his eyes but was really awake. The next thing he knew, Yeshua was gone.

With greater resolve, he decided to find something that would turn his attention from the heaviness in his eyelids. He pressed against an uncomfortable spot in the rocks. "The pain will keep me awake," he thought. No sooner did he feel its pinch against his back, than he heard Yeshua as if in a dream. He struggled to understand, and then he realized he was waking up again.

Yeshua was asking them to get up. When he stood, he saw the reason why. Torch bearing soldiers and many others were coming to the garden. Suddenly they were surrounded. The flickering light revealed Judas at the lead. Judas said something to Yeshua and embraced him. It happened so fast Peter could hardly react. The soldiers were everywhere. Yeshua stepped forward and they took him hostage. All the emotional turmoil of the evening flooded upon Peter. Before he could think, he reacted. Reaching for his concealed weapon, he struck at the closest enemy. Blood splattered Peter's face and clothes. The man screamed and lurched, grabbing his head. His severed ear fell to the ground.

Yeshua's eyes darted toward Peter. "Stop! No more of this." As Peter watched in shock, Yeshua took the bleeding ear and somehow replaced it on the man's head. It was too much. Terror filled Peter. Before his eyes, the man he took to be the next conqueror was being led away in bonds. That same man refused to fight, refused to be defended. Peter saw his dreams crumble into dust at his feet. His moment of glory would never come. He suddenly knew that Yeshua would really die, and that he might die too. The realization hit all of them like a shock wave. There was only one thing to do. Run!

And run he did. Tripping and falling in the dark. Getting scratched by brambles, bruising a shin, once almost stumbling face-first to the ground. He saw the others darting away in all directions. Then he realized that no one was chasing him. He stopped. All he could hear was his heart pounding in his ears. His breath was quick and shallow. He tried to control himself. He listened. He could see the torches of the soldiers moving away, down the hillside. There was no other sound. He was alone. In spite of the voice screaming at him to use this chance to disappear, he was compelled to follow.

Staying in the shadows, he trailed behind the captors until they entered the courtyard outside the quarters of the high priest. As he approached the doorway, he recognized one of his comrades coming out of the dark. His friend went into the courtyard with Yeshua and the soldiers. Mustering all the courage he had, Peter stood next to the doorway. He peered into the enclosure. His friend caught his eye and spoke to the doorkeeper, motioning Peter to enter. Hoping no one noticed his torn robe and the bloody bruise on his leg, he stepped into the light of the quadrant. As he moved past the slave girl who watched the door, she suddenly asked him, "You're not one of his disciples, are you?"

Caught! The adrenaline flooded his body. Trapped by his own stupidity. Why had he come here anyway? There was nothing to gain and only danger for him. The shock went through him like a napalm explosion. The girl saw him stagger ever so slightly. But as quickly as the hot flash of exposure passed over him, in the same instant he realized that there was a way of escape. The servant girl expected him to say, "No." She assumed that he wasn't one of Yeshua's followers. It was almost too easy. He did the only thing he could think of to protect himself. He tried to level his voice and speak with resolve. "Of course not."

Before she could answer or get a better look, he stepped away from the door toward the charcoal fire. There was a small group of men warming themselves, speaking in quiet voices about the events of the evening. Peter did his best to fade into the background. But any stranger in the courtyard on this particular night was bound to attract attention. Soon he noticed that two or three people sitting by the fire nodded in his direction and whispered among themselves. He was trapped again. To leave the courtyard, he would have to walk past his potential accusers and between the soldiers on guard. Surely they would come after him. He squatted down, trying to make himself as inconspicuous as possible. Under his robe, he was sweating like a pig. He felt ill. He smelled the fear on his breath. "I'll have to chance it," he thought. "If I stay here and it gets light, I'll be a prisoner for sure."

When he stood to leave the fire, one of the men in the circle noticed his bruises. It was just enough. He stared at Peter's face and asked that hideous question, "You're not one of the disciples of that man, are you?"

Peter was prepared this time. He caught the tone and used it to his advantage. The questioner was hesitant, not sure of himself. He left a little opening, just as the servant girl had. Peter took it.

"Not on your life! Do you think I am stupid?" He aimed the reproach at his adversary.

Suddenly he realized that he had spoken with a little too much bravado. Several others looked up at his reply. From the murky recesses of his memory, a face riveted itself in his view. It was the face of one of Yeshua's captors. Before Peter could turn away, the face opened its mouth.

"I've seen you before," it said to Peter. "I was there. I saw you in the garden tonight." The man spoke louder and louder as his assurance grew. Peter jerked away toward the doorway to freedom. Before he could reach the exit, several men confronted him with the slave girl in tow. They stopped him. "You *are* one of them. You're a Galilean. You speak their dialect," blurted one of the accusers. "Look here!" shouted another. "It's one of them! Look!"

It was too much. Peter tasted the vomit of fear in his throat. He shouted out, "Shut up, you !@*&#%! fools. I swear by the holy temple that I don't know this man you're talking about. A curse fall on me if I am not telling the truth. Stop bothering me, you scum, or I'll really give you something to worry about!" he said raising a fist.

As the words were falling from his lips, the crowd broke. Yeshua was being led out of the building. He raised his eyes to Peter. That look was the most painful, saddened gaze Peter had ever seen. It pierced him like a scorching fire brand. It burned into his mind to be remembered for all eternity. Peter, the once proud, the once honored, stared at Yeshua from the bottom of the cesspool.

He was covered in disgrace and shame. He was broken. Without a word, he turned his back, ran through the gate. He ran and ran until his legs collapsed, his face in the dirt weeping. His life was over. He was nothing.

The Mechanics of Guilt

Peter's encounter with guilt exemplifies what each of us face. We identify with his experience because we have had the same humiliation, desperation and shame poured upon us. In the war zones, guilt attacks us by fogging our vision of true reality. We are led to believe that guilt and shame are the same. Since we fail to see the important difference, we conclude that the emotional distress we feel in the presence of our slandered friend, our former colleague, or our deceived spouse is the psychological punishment for sinful behavior.

We think that being at fault is the same as feeling shamed. But shame is not removed by being forgiven because forgiveness reminds us that we are guilty, thus continuing the spiral. Once this confusion occurs, we are no longer open to the growth that true guilt offers.

Our difficulties with this spiritual disease begin from the fact that there are two distinct applications of the same diagnosis. Being guilty can signify a legal condition or a psychological condition. Both of these results begin as manifestations of the same activities. Both are born in an act of internal selfishness. But one leads to true guilt and an openness to reality, while the other leads to shame and blindness to reality. We must understand how this happens before we can separate these two very different consequences.

In order to grasp just how the mechanics of guilt work, we will need to take three steps in self-analysis. First, we need to expand our conceptual field. We are not interested in the limited notions of guilt such as assigning liability, breaking rules, failing promises or lapses in moral expectations. Our conceptual field must be much larger than simple legal or cultural parameters. Guilt certainly includes these constructions, but we all know that the real guts of our struggle with guilt go far beyond just breaking the rules. We are not denying that guilt has a legal foundation. What we are saying is that it is not essentially a matter of morality. There is a deeper, wider scope to this judicial application. It has to do with the essence of ego. While guilt displays symptoms within the social world, its root is really a spiritual one. Consequently, if we are to understand the foundation of guilt, we must examine what guilt says about who we really are and how we are related to God.

Secondly, we need to recognize our own proclivities toward rationalizing guilt. When we *feel* caught in the wine press of guiltiness, we often try to *think* our way out of the mess by coming up with "legitimate" excuses. We hope that adjusting the past will somehow alleviate the present. This is a futile exercise. Here we begin to confuse guilt with shame.

Guilt is associated with responsibility. It presupposes freedom. But when we *feel guilty*, we feel trapped, bound. We are not free. Even if we acknowledge blame and accept responsibility, our feelings of powerlessness continue. This form of *feeling guilty* is really shame. It is in its essence a *feeling*. It is not overcome, removed, ignored or destroyed by some mental or ethical reconstruction. It is also not eliminated by being forgiven.

When I deal with guilt in its legal application, it does not matter how I *feel* about the correct or incorrect assignment of blame. If I have committed the offense, I am to blame. I am guilty as charged. I may *feel* unjustly accused, I may *feel* as though I have excuses, but my feelings don't make any difference. Guilt is a description of the *external* assessment of responsibility.

My *feeling* guilty (shame) is an entirely different matter. Since these feelings affect my psycho-emotional well-being, they are a description of my self-assessment. They express the conclusion of my *self-evaluation*, not an acknowledgment of some external judgment of my actions. They tell me that I am untrustworthy and worthless. They attack and damage **who I am, not how I behave**. They constrict my ability to choose by making me feel helpless. Feelings of shame overpower even the pronouncement of forgiveness. This is why we keep coming back to repentance over previous sins. The shame of our past acts does not go away. We conclude that we have not truly repented because we still carry the psychological scars of those behaviors. We try again—and fail, because we *cannot be forgiven of shame*. Something else must happen to be relieved of this burden.

We need to recognize that the wholeness we seek as human beings must deal with both guilt and shame, as separate but related issues. The real mind field of guilt comes about precisely because we confuse the answers to these two conditions. We think that if we can somehow excuse our external responsibilities (blame), we will then erase our feelings of guilt (shame). What we find is that even when we experience acceptance and forgiveness (when the issue of blame has been dealt with), we continue to **feel** guilty (our shame remains unabated). Our minds have been put in order, but our emotions are not comforted. We still feel sick. What many of us have not learned is how God can take the **dangerous opportunity** of guilt in both its forms and turn it into the triumph of joy.

Recycling Versus Re-calibrating

Shame recycles. It is parasitic, living on the repetitious patterns of bestial behavior. Under the old order principles, shame returns to those past events that batter us with hopeless unworthiness. There is a circular track inside of each of us. Sometimes the loop is very short and we find ourselves back at the starting blocks before we even realize we have run the course again. Other times the loop is very long, taking years to cycle through a single circumnavigation. No matter how long it takes, at some point we end up facing the same decisions, feeling the same tension, knowing the same shame. It is the *deja vu* of our old order. Around and around we go, begging, pleading, praying, hoping that this time things will be different. But always we come back to "GO" with the same cards to play, the same dice to roll, the old future in view.

Shame is not some kind of temporary sickness like the flu. It does not attack us through some communicable social stream. It is not a trivial problem to be dealt with through modern store-shelf mental medications. And it certainly does not mean that because we feel shame, we are really only sick people in need of mental readjustment. Shame is not a figment of our overly strained mental imaginations. It will not go away by adopting a positive attitude toward life. We feel shame because we are guilty. As long as guilt exists, shame must continue.

What, then, can we do about guilt? First, we must see that guilt is not a genetic infection. It does not arrive fully formed in our personality makeup. It is not the hereditary gift of our parents. Guilt is an integral part of the entire old order. It is a toxic condition like air pollution. We encounter it from the moment of birth and we live under its influence all our days. Humanity has brought it upon itself. We make deliberate decisions that produce patterns of smog-thinking. These patterns become repetitious and automatic. Those that are not based on the true reality create infection with lethal consequences. In particular, all addictions produce guilt and the Beast uses this fact to introduce us to the debilitating arena of shame.

If we abuse our physical bodies, we will suffer the consequences. The same is true of our psychological and spiritual makeup. If we live falsely, we will suffer greatly. There will be remissions – periods when we believe that we have conquered our own internal mechanics, when things seem to be moving ahead. But before too long, the fatigue will return. Spiritual and psychological breathing will become more and more difficult. We find ourselves back at Square One. We will once again have the masks torn away and know that we are dying. Eventually, inevitably, guilt and shame will kill us.

In order to break this recycling phenomenon, we must clearly understand the difference between guilt and shame. **Shame** is the debilitating, inwardly focused emotional nausea that accompanies my feelings of self-worthlessness with a loss of dignity as a consequence of some prior irresponsible act. It is intensified in the presence of those offended or injured by my irresponsibility, whether they are other human beings or God. The critical point about shame is that it *cannot be forgiven*.

Since shame attacks who I am, it is of no consequence to my self-identity to be told that I have been forgiven of the action that perpetrated this dysfunctional self-evaluation. Shame continues unabated because it is not about my behavior but rather about my being. It automatically destroys my freedom, even the freedom to accept forgiveness.

My personal experience with shame was the single biggest factor that kept me on the addictive track. When I felt the barrage of shame overwhelming me, I forgot about God's provision of forgiveness. I thought of myself as unworthy, and consequently, I gave myself permission in my unworthiness to continue the behavior that brought about my guilt and shame. Shame does not go away when I am forgiven. Therefore, I told myself that I was doomed to *feeling* guilty, so I might as well continue with the addiction. The result was continuing the cycle. **I lost the freedom to be forgiven.**

True guilt is not about who I am. It is about how responsible or irresponsible my actions are. In the new order, this is the same as saying that guilt is about whether or not my choices are aligned with the character of God. Often, we think of guilt as the antonym of innocence, but this polarity conceals the true purpose of guilt in the new order setting. Guilt is the flip side of righteousness. Guilt describes our status apart from the redeeming work of God. It is the shorthand way of saying that God is holy, man is not holy and, therefore, relationship between these two persons is broken.

The correct polarity is not guilt and innocence. It is rather guilt and righteousness; the difference in relationship status between man and God.

Consequently, guilt is not primarily an ethical or moral quality. It is rather a statement of relationship before God. The biblical documents argue that ethical and moral precepts and legislation can do nothing more for humanity's relationship with God than continue to bind men under the power of the performance principle (I am only worth as much as I do), a principle that draws its strength from the old order and always leads to death (Romans 2 and 3). This is why Yeshua taught that we can never **earn** God's grace or favor. The very act of appeasement is an act motivated by the Beast, because it still requires that self is in control of the process.

In God's new order, guilt is the precursor, not for increased moral fervor, but for the replacement of human effort with the obedient acknowledgment of God's unmerited liberating act and proclamation. In the domain of spiritual re-engineering, I have been found guilty because I have acted in ways that resulted in my personal misalignment with God. The remedy for guilt is God's forgiveness through and because of the responsible, unselfish act of Yeshua. In other words, I am not rescued because *I* do something, but rather because *he* was faithful in what *he* did.

While the provision for this remedy depends **solely** on God's completed act, its application to me depends on my personal repentance. Thus, the new order kingdom sees the concept of guilt as a critical step in self-awareness. Guilt is **necessary** in order for us to realize that repentance is needed to repair the right-standing relationship (righteousness) before God. Guilt is **necessary** in order for me to understand that I cannot repair this right-standing relationship myself but must rely completely on God to act on my behalf. Finally, guilt is **necessary** to correct my vision of reality so that I will refocus from the strangulation of the performance principle to the liberation of God's unwavering promise to bring His people into alignment with Him. Guilt has spiritual purpose. It is intended to draw our attention to God's faithfulness and to elicit our loyalty and obedience to Him. <u>The intention of guilt is to recalibrate my focus – to direct me away from my independent self-in-control attitude toward my dependent acknowledgment on God's graciousness.</u>

When I repent and God forgives, He changes my **status** from guilty to righteous. I am not considered *innocent*. Instead, I become aware of my newly confirmed status—repentant and forgiven—in spite of my guilt; a status that depends entirely on God's character, not mine. My changed status means that I am now a family member of His community living under the promises of His covenant, desiring to be obedient to His reality. I am not innocent, but neither am I condemned.

Shame robs me of this critical self-awareness. Shame questions my worth and attacks me by convincing me that **I am still unlovable as I am and I will forever be that way because this is who I am**. Shame recycles my irresponsibility, continuing to keep me aligned with the old order because it refuses to acknowledge that God loves me in spite of my guiltiness, that God loves me **exactly as I am**. Shame uses the awareness of my lack of *innocence* to convince me that I am still condemned. Shame isolates me from community with my fellow human beings and from participation in the covenant community with God. Shame propagates the performance principle at the same time that it alienates me from any possibility of fulfillment of its demands. Its attack on my self-worth is exhaustive and complete. I am left utterly alone and unlovable.

You might conclude that this is intolerable, and as a result, I would immediately reject such debilitating thinking. But that isn't the case. Once shame has convinced me that I am no good, oddly enough I find solace in this unworthiness. It *removes* me from responsibility. If I truly am worthless, then it really doesn't matter what I do. Therefore, I numb my feelings with addictive behavior and *feel justified* in doing so. After all, I am only taking care of myself when no one else wants to. The vicious cycle continues because shame is *comforting* as long as I can remove the feelings of guilt that should accompany my behavior.

Self Again

The paradox of shame parallels the paradox of fear. Shame seeks to isolate me from the God who would forgive by convincing me that I am, once again, different. Instead of a positive polarity of difference (being better than others), I am drawn into a negative polarity. Shame convinces me that I am worse than others—that no one could really love me if they only knew who I am. Shame convinces me that my secret sins are unlike anyone else's. This negative polarity is no less narcissistic than the fear that forgets God. Locked in the shame of saying, "I'm no good" or "I'm worthless," I am still focused entirely on me. Self is still at the center. The Beast is alive and well even in the midst of our self-degradation. No wonder forgiveness cannot break the log jam of shame. To accept forgiveness is to admit the powerlessness of self – precisely what shame cannot do.

When we deal with guilt in the true sense, we are forced to acknowledge responsibility. Guilt is God's **purposeful** dangerous opportunity to lead us to forgiveness and to a relationship with Him. Guilt leads us away from ourselves and toward confrontation with God. Guilt recalibrates our powerlessness, driving us toward God's care. With true guilt in our peripheral vision, we are asked to focus on the reality of God's kingdom permeated with forgiveness. Guilt ultimately leads us to God's love for us and His affirmation of our worth, not on the basis of self-in-control but on the basis of self-out-of-control.

Guilt and God

Ultimately guilt occurs as a result of an offense to God. Guilt is the product of sin. No matter what the secondary symptoms are (such as broken human relationships, material abuses or selfish inconsistency), guilt is finally a matter that must be addressed to God.

David knew this when he was confronted about his adultery and murder. His psalm (Psalm 51) confesses his guilt solely before God, even though he clearly harmed many other human beings with his actions. David saw that the root of his selfishness was an offense to God; that it had to be dealt with at that level before any other amends could be made. God's holiness is the driving force behind all new-order life. When our vision is expanded to reveal the true character of the world we occupy, we must first acknowledge that our actions and reactions have consequences for a much larger picture than the scope of our lives. We are players in God's orchestra. Consequently, when I sin, the first person I hurt is God. The second is myself.

On the evening that Peter experienced the guilt and shame of denial and failure, this experience was more than self-protection or betrayal. Even though Peter did not understand the full role of Yeshua as Messiah, he at least understood this: Yeshua was a very special man, anointed by God Himself (Peter witnessed that). Yeshua claimed to be the Messiah (Peter said that). Yeshua had power over nature (it was Peter who climbed from the boat and walked on the water to Yeshua). And finally, Yeshua predicted Peter's terrible experience would happen. Although he did not know it all, he certainly knew that Yeshua was someone absolutely unique and wonderful.

Imagine the amplification of his shame when Peter witnessed Yeshua's resurrection. Of course, he was overjoyed to know that Yeshua had come back to life. The exhilaration swept over him and the others like a tidal wave. But something else happened at the same time. His shame returned. He recycled. At least when Yeshua was dead, Peter could punish himself into anesthetic numbness. He could pretend to forget. But not now. Now the man he betrayed was alive.

We can suffer shame about our behavior concerning those who are no longer part of our lives, but the intensity diminishes as the departure grows. Eventually we stop crying. We perform self-anesthesia. Peter did not have even this consolation. Yeshua was alive again. Every time Peter looked at him, or thought about him, or heard someone speak his name, the courtyard flashed before his mind. A twinge of pain stabbed the back of his head. His eyes filled with suppressed tears. Peter understood as well as anyone of us can ever understand, what it must be like to be constantly reminded of personal relationship failure. Peter hated himself for what he was – guilty, unforgiven and ashamed.

So we find him, *after* the joy of the resurrection, *after* the appearances of Yeshua, returning to his ignoble beginnings. He was Simon again. A simple fisherman. No longer worthy. No longer proud. Back to his roots, trying to forget about this episode in his life. Just to make himself numb.

But Yeshua would not leave him alone even in his humiliation. All night long on the boat trying to do the same old things the same old way, Peter found that he was not the same old person. He had changed. His old life was no longer routine. He had lost the knack of fishing along with the desire. The morning came. On the shore a man called to the boat. They recognized the voice. It was Yeshua.

Peter's agony and inner turmoil burst from him. He had to face Yeshua and himself. Without waiting for the boat to return to the edge of the sea, he jumped overboard and swam to Yeshua. He was ready to stand accused. He had to clear this sickness from his soul. Yeshua was ready too.

The Three and Three

Two men standing over a cooking fire. The smell of fish, the lake, the cool breeze mixed with opposing emotions in the fisherman. He wanted to fall to his knees and beg forgiveness. At the same time, he feared the humiliation of Yeshua's gaze. Shame caught him between remorse and pride and immobilized him. Yeshua led Peter by the psychological hand to the place of forgiveness. He asked Peter the critical question, "Simon, son of John, do you love me more than these?"

There are several critical issues that we must keep in mind as we see how Yeshua dealt with Peter's guilt. The first is Yeshua's address, "Simon, son of John." Using the name "Simon" places this conversation in the midst of the habitual world of the fisherman. Here is the old Simon, fishing again, just as Yeshua found him when he first called him to follow. There is no immediate attempt to place the restoration process in the transformed world of "Peter."

Restoration begins with who we are where we are – just ordinary people in ordinary life. Guilt is part of the old order. Feeling guilty is a death sentence that stems from old-order principles. The fact and the feeling can't be dealt with by simply making a mental jump to God's side of the boat. <u>God's reality therapy must begin precisely at the point where we suffer.</u> God does not ask us to be something other than who we are, but He does ask us to be truthful about who we are.

"Simon, son of John" is a formal address. This opening announces something serious. This is not a "slap-on-the-back," "Everything-is-going-to-be-okay," "Let's-be-friends-again," conversation. This is solemn, important, significant. It's going to deal not only with who we are as individuals, but who we are as products of the broken human race. When God speaks to us personally about the guilt in our existence, He is absolutely serious. Pay attention. Something important is about to happen.

Peter must have taken one of those short breaths when he heard this address. The old name, the family line. He steeled himself for the accusation. He was ready to admit his failure. But the accusation never came. Instead he heard a question, "Do you love me more than these?"

Our translations of these passages at the end of John's gospel cannot capture the subtlety of this question or of Peter's answer for we have only a single word for love.[18] In Greek there are three

---

[18]Various scholars argue that the change in Greek words for "love" found in this passage are nothing more than the characteristic stylistic variations of John. I find this argument unconvincing for it assumes that John was unaware of the theological import of such changes. Such an assumption is in contrast to the entire thematic emphasis of John's gospel where theological concerns outweigh even chronological accuracy. However, even if these scholars are correct, and we

common expressions for love: *agape, eros* and *phileo. Agape* is love without conditions, love that reaches into the depths of being, love associated with the touch of the divine. *Eros* is love connected with possession, love motived by self-desire. *Phileo* is love in friendship and brotherly bonds.

Yeshua asked Peter, "Do you love (*agape*) me more than these?" He was asking for Peter's unconditional commitment to Yeshua as his Lord. Buried in the question was the reminder of Peter's own proclamation of unfailing loyalty. Yeshua asked for Peter's renewal of commitment after all that had happened, after all the pain, the denial, the humiliation. Yeshua asked Peter to search himself and know who he really was. Was he the man who determined to follow Yeshua? Or was he just a simple fisherman with a failed-life vision? Was he for God or for self?

The first step in conquering guilt is a true reality check. Who are you? "Are you the one I believe you to be?" asks God. Or are you the one you have chosen to become? "Will you believe in the person I have called you to be, or will you withdraw into the person you feel that you are?"

Peter's answer shows the depth of his despair. "Lord, you know that I love (*phileo*) you." God brings us face-to-face with the reality of ourselves. In that encounter we often hope for renewal but cannot bring ourselves to let go of the past failures.

---

cannot make theological points out of this change in the Greek words, the actions taken by Yeshua and the response of Peter still demonstrate outward focus as essential to forgiveness and renewal.

We compromise ourselves. Our shame robs us of releasing the inner person God knows we were intended be. "Yes, Lord, I love you, but I can't bring myself to say it without conditions. Look what happened to me when I did that before. I failed. I am afraid to fail again. I can't let go of that awful self-hatred for what I did. I can't admit that there is a twisted comfort in this self-loathing. I am ashamed and ashamed to be ashamed." Even when we hope to be the whole person God calls, we find our emotional feet mired in old-order quicksand. We sink as we stand.

Yeshua did not answer with a reprimand. He did not accuse. He did not ask for apology or penance. He called Peter to the new order all over again. "Care for my lambs." Become the fisher of men that I know you can be. Move from the inner recycling prison of your shame to the outward reality of God's kingdom. Surrender yourself and be healed. Reach out to another from your own pain and find love for yourself through selflessness. Yeshua called Peter to *outward* manifestation, not inner psychological battles.

Yeshua teaches Peter two fundamental insights about shame. First, shame operates with total inward myopia. It lives in a hall of mirrors. As long as we stare into its reflection, we cannot see the world as it is, as God sees it. In a hall of mirrors, we can only see the selfishness we feel. Secondly, shame is a subtle way of saying that I am still the center of my universe. Shame lets me delude myself into thinking I am special; worse, but still different than all others. Shame removes me from being one of God's many creatures.

Yeshua takes Peter through the process again. "Simon, son of John, do you love (*agape*) me?" Again, Peter is reminded of his personal tragedy. Again, the guilt is placed in the ordinary world of "Simon." Again, Yeshua asks for thorough and honest self-evaluation. Yeshua intends to let Peter forgive himself for the three denials by performing three affirmations. God understands that both guilt and shame must be confronted.

Peter responds with the same answer. "You know that I love (*phileo*) you." Yeshua gives no criticism. He directs Peter toward the new reality. He points Peter toward the act of selfless giving that will shatter the bonds of shame. "Shepherd my sheep."

Yeshua poses the inevitable third question. Peter knew that it was coming. The pattern had been indelibly marked in his mind from the moment the final curse left his lips on that terrible evening. But something happened between the second and third question. Yeshua moved from the place of divine, unconditional love to stand on Peter's ground. "Simon, son of John, do you love (*phileo*) me?"

Yeshua adopted Peter's expression of love. Removed from the realm of the unconditional, the implied commitment remains. Yeshua says, "I know your pain. I know your uncertainty. I know your shame. But I want your affirmation. And you need to know that I will accept *your* affirmation."

The Gospel records that Peter was grieved because Yeshua asked the third time. The point of healing had come. Three times denied, three times affirmed, three times forgiven. And three times reminded that shame produces inward turning when God requires outward giving. "Tend my sheep," came Yeshua's reply.

Peter suffered not only from the need to be forgiven for his failure, he also suffered from the collapse of self-worth. Yeshua allowed Peter the opportunity to reconstitute the proclamation of his loyalty. But simply reaffirming his faithfulness to Yeshua was not enough to break the grip of his shame.

The Focus of Forgiveness

Yeshua could have come to Peter and simply pronounced him forgiven, but he knew that more is involved than simple pardon. God has, in essence, given each of us this opportunity to change our status. In His court, we are acquitted because we are shielded by the faithfulness of the Messiah. The legal issue has been settled. But that alone is not enough for us. It is not enough because our emotional distress is not only about our failed responsibilities. It is about our shame, our internal conclusion of worthlessness. To deal with that, God must show us the true reality. He must open our minds to the vision of the new order so that we can see that guilt has been forgiven and that shame is without foundation.

If God values me so much that He is willing and anxious to forgive me of my real guilt (the offense against Him), then who is it that can possibly hold me shamed? Only me. And only because I am focused on myself, my own pain, my own misery. I am my own whipping boy, ready to beat myself for my own needs, pretending that I am not at the center of my own world because I feel so bad about me, seeking comfort in the arms of the Beast who wishes to kill me.

To that God says, "Open your eyes. See my world. Tend to my business." There is no room for selfish self-abasement in this kingdom because such activity presumes that God holds us guilty. **And He has proclaimed that He does not!**

Yeshua confronted Peter in this self-withdrawal. God faces us with the same question. Do we love Him more than we love the self-flagellation? Are we ready to put aside the old order and its paralyzing auto-anesthesia? Are we willing to leave **us** behind and reach out to **them** just because He asks it?

Guilt dies when God forgives. Shame is made impotent when we see the world from the perspective of God's reality. This can never happen as long as we are trapped in the emotional baggage that turns us in upon ourselves. We will only **be** forgiven and **feel** forgiven when we **act** out God's love by choosing to believe that what God says about who we are is true.

Shame requires that we hide within ourselves. God has pulled away the covering and exposed us. God is willing for the dangerous opportunity of guilt to wage war within us so that we can awaken to His reality. That reality is emblazoned with **FORGIVENESS**. Forgiveness is what is real. All the rest is self-delusion. All the rest is the den of the Beast.

God has already taken away our guilt. We are the only ones holding on to it. Now He asks us to act on the basis of His character, not ours. To act on the faithfulness of His promise, not ours. To act on the strength of His righteousness, not ours. To act on the constancy of His mercy, not ours. **TO ACT ON HIS LOVE!** To forgive because He has pronounced us forgiven. And leave the dry lifeless bones of guilt and shame behind.

180

CHAPTER TEN

The Holy Reversal

"What is that to us?   See to that yourself."
(Matthew 27:4)

It has taken a long time to get to the center of the battle. Now we are at ground zero. After we have been pummeled by fear, we discover courage in God's faithfulness. After we have been poured out by shame, we find forgiveness in God's righteousness. But we still must face the hideous strength of the final war zone. This is the deepest recess of the Beast's lair, the central command of the old order, the last to fall, the hardest to overcome.

Although it often appears less odious, pride is really the "my way highway." It is the epitome of everything that the Beast stands for. It is the quintessential statement of the old-order principles because it is completely opposed to God's logic. God's logic is the holy reversal, the upside-down nature of true reality. God works in ways that are completely backwards from bestial logic, the topsy-turvy solution to how we think about the world.

God's way is not our way. God wants humility; we want heroes. God wants weakness; we want strength. God wants submission; we want glorification. God wants contrition; we want self-esteem. God wants repentance; we want rewards. God wants servants; we want status. God wants listeners: we want orators. God wants promises; we want patronizing. God wants meekness; we want admiration. God wants gentleness; we want power. God wants mercy; we want advantage. God wants purity; we want platitudes. God wants righteousness; we want to be proven right. God wants quiet accomplishments; we want fame.

Just as we found that God's operational plans are the upside-down logic of our way of seeing things, now we discover that the real connectivity with God has nothing to do with my gain but rather with my emptiness. Instead of God giving to me, I am called to give to Him. Instead of God blessing me, I am called to offer myself as a blessing to Him. Instead of receiving a divine purpose for me, I am asked to participate in His divine purpose. When the last layers of self-in-control are peeled away, the heart of the matter is my acceptance of God's request that I give Him what is due – the very self that He has created me to be. So the final line in the logic of God must read like this: where we want fullness, God wants emptiness.

Gethsemane III

For the last few months the tension had been almost unbearable. Every time the group needed to make even the smallest purchase, he agonized that one of the others would question where the money had gone. So he kept to himself. He wasn't inclined to be outspoken anyway. For as long as he could remember, small sins had plagued him until they grew to be living inkblots, publicly staining his character. More than once he had run from those who found him out. But he always knew how to survive. That was it. He was a survivor. He didn't

182

need anyone. He could take care of himself. Maybe it was his upbringing. Maybe it was the need to always be on guard. He had learned early that no one really cared, really understood. No one could really be trusted with his soul. Yet, somehow, he thought that this time it would be different. The leader seemed so confident, so unruffled by those around him, as though he were looking into a different dimension when he saw the same barren hillsides they traveled together.

That alone would have been enough attraction. But when this man actually invited *him* to join his special company, the call was irresistible. Finally, here was someone who didn't care about the mistakes of the past. Finally, he met someone who seemed to put unbreakable trust back into his life.

"But the past is never erased, is it?" thought Judas to himself. Even when Jesus seemed to be the perfect answer to all of those internal struggles Judas had carried for years, it turned out to be just another pipe dream.

Judas stood by the door to the second-floor stairway as his mind paced itself through the last three years. He remembered how hopeful he had been when that call came to him. A new start. A chance to begin again. And not alone, but with a recognized leader who had already gathered some respect for his miraculous works. What joy he had felt those first few months. What power he had seen. How wonderful it was to feel the envy of those poor hundreds who tried to get close to Jesus but couldn't. *He* was one of the chosen.

Then the trouble started. He had only himself to blame at first. A few coins held aside just for his personal use. It was really a petty amount and, after all, look at the indignity they had to suffer at the hands of those hypocritical spiritual charlatans. So he took just a pittance for himself, just for a little something to ease his troubled mind. He was just trying to survive.

No one really knew. He had done it countless times before he joined this rag-tailed band of no-accounts. Actually, now that he really thought about it, any one of them might have done the same had they been given the opportunity. Just watching out for old Number One. What was the harm in that?

Of course, he had to admit that he might have overstepped the bounds occasionally. If he had just been a little more discreet. A little more cautious. But then they were the ones who put him in charge of the funds, weren't they? And if they were that stupid, then they deserved whatever they got.

That incident with the perfume, though, that was a real blunder. It still rankled him as he thought about that whore being given such honor. Here he had trundled along behind this spineless merchant of doom for three years, watching him excite the crowds to near frenzy with his magical powers only to see him run off to hide in the desert. How many times had he endured the personal humiliation of Yeshua's refusal to step up to the challenge? Why didn't he use that power he had to drive out the scum of Rome and set up a real kingdom, one with power and glory? How many times had he pleaded with Yahweh to get this leader in line? Then they could all be wealthy, secure, important.

But, no, that wasn't good enough for this Messiah! Instead he spent his time with the losers. He even had that hated Matthew as part of the group. What an insult! Too bad it would end now, before Matthew could be humiliated for his past allegiance. At least the personal affront of association with that low-life bastard would soon be finished. It was just dumb luck that Matthew never kept track of the funds. He certainly knew how. But he was under the leader's spell just like the rest of them – still thinking that the dream would come true.

"Not me," Judas muttered out loud. His own voice surprised him. "This really is getting to me," he thought. Soon enough it would be finished and he could get on with his life. Three years wasted on this crusade. Not soon enough to get out. Not one day soon enough.

Judas bristled. His thoughts returned to the whore. It was possible that Yeshua really liked the woman. She certainly was attractive and probably great in bed. But anyone who intends to lead a nation can't be dragging common street whores around with him. Yeshua should have waited just a little longer. Once they had the upper hand, he could have had any woman he wanted.

It was so humiliating. Under those circumstances, complaining about the waste of money was justified. "If only that damn tax collector hadn't been so quick to give me the eye," he muttered. That had nearly done it, right there. It took every cunning fiber in his being to get them off the subject of expenses once he blurted out his complaint. But he prevailed. He bluffed them all. To this very day, no one really knew.

The wind whipped around Judas' tunic. He pulled it closer to gather in his body warmth. He hated to wait. All his life he had hated waiting. Being part of the masses. Being treated like the common garbage that most people were. "That's what it really came down to," he thought. He just couldn't take the disgrace of being unrecognized. Those early days held so much promise. Now that he looked back on them, even he had been duped.

Anger shot through him now as he recalled those incidents when James and John and Simon were given special consideration. How could Yeshua have been so blind? Of all the possibilities, why would he choose two half-wit brothers who were nothing but Mama's boys and that oaf of a fisherman? That guy was so stupid he didn't even know when to shut his own mouth.

Judas remembered his humiliation when those three returned from the mountain top. They couldn't stop talking about this vision thing they had seen. Why on earth would Yeshua overlook the chance of putting someone in the inner circle who really knew how to use power? Someone like him. At least he had the satisfaction of seeing that buffoon Simon put in his place with the conversation about Elijah. Judas had enjoyed that. Especially since his answer to the question was wrong.

Buying a few favors with what's-her-name had helped him forget too. There was something very satisfying about secretly knowing that he was using the same money that Simon had been given to get a little for himself.

Now that he reflected on the disappointments that had led him to this night, he realized that none of the petty incidents with the other followers had really pushed him over the edge. Of course, it was nice to know that he was about to put them all in their places. But none of them were the real cause. They were all such sheep. Lead, follow or get out of the way. That was his motto. And those other eleven certainly needed to get out of the way.

No, now that he thought about it, the real culprit was Yeshua. If anyone were to blame for this night, it was Yeshua himself. How many times had Yeshua made promises that he did not keep? "I will give you living water so that you will never thirst." "My yoke is easy and my burden light." "I have come that you might live life abundantly." Now, after three years of waiting, where was the living water that an army could use to cross the desert without thirst? Where was the victory to make burdens light? Where was the life of wealth and pleasure and abundance?

Nowhere! Nothing! Not a single promise kept! It sounded great. It looked great when the crowds stirred with anticipation. But in the end, Yeshua got hung up on martyrdom.

By the time they came to Jerusalem, Judas had made up his mind. He had to get out. His possible exposure was getting more and more risky. He actually ran into one of his suppliers just that week. Fortunately, the others thought that he was simply discussing arrangements for food when he stopped to talk to the man. In the city, anything could happen.

Besides, the whole scheme was collapsing around him. It certainly wasn't his fault that their one-time leader was going schizo on them. First Yeshua marched into the temple and beat the hell out of those moneychangers. Judas reached into his inside pocket and felt the glow of a few of the coins he had "rescued" from the temple floor. Yeshua had the whole city buzzing with great expectations. Then he began to talk about his death wish. What pap! How was he supposed to inspire confidence in the masses when he went around talking about death all the time? That really confirmed Judas' suspicions. The man just couldn't cut it. Time to take the money and run.

That's when Judas realized how he might turn this personal disgrace into a little profit. This should never have had to happen if Yeshua had only consulted him about making it to the top. Judas knew the ways of the world. A little here, a little there, and pretty soon people were under your control. Sheep. That's what Yeshua had called them and he was right. But they were sheep to be used, not to be given gifts that belonged to the more deserving. Yeshua had lost it when he confused benevolence with benefit.

It was great to be kind to the sheep, but there was a limit to compassion and charity. Heaven knows that all those sheep were ready to do whatever he asked. They would have gladly sacrificed themselves if he had only given them a vision of a new regime. Judas knew it. He felt it as he had felt nothing else in his life. "Yeshua should have done it my way," he thought. But instead of the strategy of powerful comrades, Yeshua spoke of being servants. How ridiculous! No one ever got anything by being a slave. The rich get richer and the poor get poorer. That was the real way of the world.

Judas flicked his eyes to the right when he heard the scrape of sandals on the stone. There he was, coming along the alleyway. Judas stepped from the door just as the man passed. As he came up behind the messenger, he whispered, "Evening, friend." The man jumped as if he had seen a spirit.

"You startled me," he replied.

"You can never be too cautious, you know. No one watches your back for you."

Without another word, they strode off into the dark. Soon they came to the courtyard of the high priest. Judas stepped over the sill and ducked inside.

Pride

Pride is about human strength. It is the fundamental desire of every one of us to assert ourselves above our fellows. It starts with the conviction that I am the only one who *really* cares about me. When Yeshua suggested that the we need to become like children in order to enter into the kingdom of heaven, he had the root problem of pride in mind.

Children feel their dependence. It is so ubiquitous to their very being that they are almost unconscious of it. They glory in their weakness. They must depend on someone else to survive. Our modern world is confronted by this reality every time we view the desperate plight of the Third World children of this planet. Without someone bigger, stronger, wiser to depend on, children die. That is the cold, hard fact of life. Children cannot afford the luxury of pride. When we leave childhood behind, we lose more than naiveté. We lose our sense of *complete* dependence. We learn to sing with Frank Sinatra. We convince ourselves that we can do it our way.

Before we raise any objections to this line of thought, we must carefully consider several distinctions that commonly obscure the root problem of pride. The first is our training that we should be proud of who we are – that pride is an essential element of self-worth. This is absolutely true. It is true simply because it is grounded in the fact that God has provided the foundation of our worthiness in the declaration that He loves us as we are.

But this is not a foundation that we earned or deserved. It is not a right of being human. We did not wrest this condition from a hostile universe. We did not pull ourselves up to be slightly less than angels by our own efforts. We did nothing to deserve this confirmation of our eternal worth. The facts are quite the opposite. From God's perspective, we actually went about trying to destroy the very efforts He took to grant us this status.

Therefore, it is justifiable to be proud of the confirmation of our unconditional worth and to feel the resulting strength from knowing that we are loved as we are. But pride in this position is not and cannot be in ourselves. It is pride that can only be associated with being a child of God—of being confirmed worthy because we have chosen to be utterly dependent. Proud to be called one of His is the spiritual equivalent of saying "for thine is the power and the kingdom and the glory forever and ever." It can be no other way.

Secondly, we must be sure that we are not confusing the symptomatic use of pride with its bestial manifestation. We may rightly describe ourselves as being proud of our efforts, of our children, of our achievements or a host of other activities and relationships. When I say that I am proud of my wife's tenacity in her pursuit of a career, I do not imply that I have ignored the hand of God guiding her life. Nor do I mean that she has the right to claim that by her efforts alone she is what she is. If she describes herself as proud of her achievements, that does not mean that she would not ascribe her success to God's purpose and direction. The proof of this comes in our failures. When the world crashes in on our best laid plans, those of us who ascribe to symptomatic pride will still feel the strength of God's care, the compassion of His love. We will know that whether we live in good times or bad, He has not abandoned us. His faithfulness is the only sure foundation of our belief in ourselves.

Bestial pride has very different results. The Beast lives in a dark world separate from the Creator God. His form of pride asserts itself apart from God's foundation of worthiness. It results in resistance to God's grace and God's will. It is the central core of the old order precisely because it is the final stronghold of willful independence from the Creator. In Biblical terms, it is the denial of God's authority, majesty and glory.

This form of pride says that **I** am the only *final* authority for my life, that **I** am the only real king of my realm, that **I** am the only one truly deserving of my worship. This pride violates the central focus of the entire created universe by usurping the role of God. It quite deliberately says, "I am my own god. My life is what it is because I have made it so. I need nothing and no one to become what I choose to be. I am the most important thing in my universe." This is the essence of self-in-control. No matter how disguised we attempt to make it, no matter how much we try to rationalize it, no matter what we do to justify it, the simple fact is this: if self is in control, God is not.

Spirituality is digital. We are either aligned with God's grace or we are not. The old order and the new order mix about as easily as oil and water. There is no compromise possible here. <u>Prideful self-delusion is nothing more than a disguised decision to resist God's prompting to change.</u>

Most of us will recoil at this bold expression of the essence of bestial pride. We will say to ourselves that we are not like that. We will feel the immediate affront that this egotism expresses. We will claim humility as a part of our character. For most of us, these reactions are entirely correct. The fact is that our lives are not usually lived in such flagrant opposition to interdependence and humility. But our repulsion associated with this brazen description of the pride of the Beast only masks the insidious nature of this final soul disease.

The Judas Syndrome

If we look back at our semi-fictitious story about Judas, we will see how self-concealing pride can be. Judas was probably not the heinous creature that popularized versions of the Gospel story have led us to believe. He was not the devil incarnate, the personification of evil or demon possessed. Certainly, Yeshua chose him as one of the disciples because Yeshua saw him as one more example of God's broken children in need of redemption – but more than that. A rabbi chose a disciple because he saw great potential in the man. Yeshua must have seen that in Judas – great potential to be a mighty servant of the Lord. If these cautions aren't kept in mind, we will be inclined to write off the person of Judas as someone so alien that there is nothing for us to learn from his failure to find reconciliation with God. This is important, for if we should make an *a priori* decision to relegate Judas to the human damned, we will blind ourselves to how much he is **exactly like us**.

Judas is a man with some very common human frailties. He does not know forgiveness because he has not learned repentance. Small sins overtake him precisely because he has not voluntarily placed his recognized failures in the hands of God. He acknowledges no dependence on the Father. He is the resistant child.

The Judas of our story has determined that the evidence of this world confirms his isolation. He believes that he is alone in the fight to become fulfilled. Ultimately this belief means that he lives according to the rules of separation from God the Father. The Beast dominates and controls his thinking and his behavior.

Consequently, in spite of the fact that he entertains the resident human hope that someone other than himself will validate his worth, he has come to the conclusion that no one except himself can give him purpose and meaning. When left in existential isolation, human beings are unable to love themselves. So we see Judas thinking just like many of us think. Look out for Number One. Do unto others before they do unto you. No one really loves me. Others are only trying to use me. I am alone in the world. I cannot trust others. Once bitten, twice shy.

Are these thoughts so alien to any one of us? Common experiences say not. Yet they are the direct result of resistance to God's role as Father. They deny His care. They spurn His love. They refuse His purpose. They reject His authority. They flow directly from the proposition that I am my own self-sufficient, independent center of significance.

More importantly, the extension of operating on these beliefs leads directly to an entire litany of bestial pride behaviors. We see these in Judas when he desires the *envy* of others ("to feel the envy of those poor hundreds"). We see it in the *rationalization of sin* ("it was really a petty amount"). We see it in the *denial of responsibility* ("What was the harm in that?"). We see it in the *aversion to personal humiliation* ("How many times had he endured"). We see it in the *misunderstanding of God's intention* ("he pleaded with Yahweh to get this leader in line"). We see it in *discrimination and hatred of God's other children* ("that hated Matthew," "those sheep," "the common garbage," "Get out of the way"). We see it in *avarice and greed* ("be wealthy," "could have any woman he wanted," "real power"). We see it in the *desire for glorification and status* ("the disgrace of being unrecognized"). We see it in the *enjoyment of others' suffering* ("put them all in their places"). Finally, we see it in the *rejection of the role of servant* ("no one ever got anything by being a slave").

Are these characteristics only applicable to the single person of Judas? Are they alien to our daily life? No! What makes them so hideous is that they are about us! We are all infected with the Judas syndrome. We must not forget our commonality with those same people who cheered Yeshua on Palm Sunday and clamored for his crucifixion five days later. They are us! When we allow the evil strength of the Beast to fill us with envy, denial, discrimination, greed, power, self-justification and a host of other egocentric manifestations, we put ourselves in the place of Judas, seeking personal advantage, rejecting the call to be God's servant for the desire of our own way.

Judas was not some devil disguised as a human being. He was simply the representative extension of what we are when we refuse to confront our brokenness. He betrayed Yeshua because he sought to save his own life, to reward himself, to gain personal advantage. Have we not done the same, time after time?

The End of Pride

Since this is the case, what has God to say about our desperate condition? We all know that evil triumphed in the person of Judas. That triumph did not occur when he betrayed Yeshua. The most despicable act on earth became the most wonderful blessing of heaven. God turned Yeshua's betrayal into Messiah's victory. Evil triumphed in Judas' life not in the courtyard of the high priest nor in the Garden, but rather when he destroyed himself in separation from God. The ultimate conclusion of any old-order operation is the destruction of one of God's children.

This is the final tragedy. Judas could have been forgiven. God is faithful. God is merciful. He will receive His children back to Himself with open arms if only they will come. But Judas would not.

The tragedy of pride is that it destroys the value of what God has created. Pride begins this lethal attack on us by first separating us from knowing God's forgiveness. Without His forgiveness, we experience human isolation. The cancer of separation from God entails separation from those who would express God's love to us. Isolation brings the agony of worthlessness. The more we fight to gain self-justifying worth, the less we are able to hold it. In the end, our internal mathematics show our lives as counting for nothing. Death merely completes the arithmetic. Another zero added to a column of zeros.

God denounces pride. Not because He commands subservience from His creation, but because pride kills the very essence of the glory that He has created. God denounces pride by telling us that He loves. He loves *us*. And as a result of His love for us, He forgives. Bestial pride cannot exist in harmony with love, for the one demands that I be the center of my existence and the other demands that I give up my ownership of self for the sake of another. Real love is self-sacrificing. Real love has experienced firsthand, the fallacy of gain through acquisition.

Since real love knows that it can only find fulfillment by giving itself away without the calculation of gain, it is logically, emotionally and theologically **incompatible** with self-in-control. It cannot exist in the same universe as the self-operating on the belief that what I have must be retained, and what I want must be taken.

Emptiness Again

The paradigm model of the antithesis between love and pride is seen in the result of that single night in Gethsemane. God's love was demonstrated in giving for us. If anyone had the right to pride, it would have been Yeshua. Even the Father proclaimed that He was pleased with His Son. But pride is incompatible with love. Love is essentially the action of the servant. It is most vividly expressed in the act of forgiveness.

Yeshua recognized the centrality of forgiveness, not only as the active expression of God's love but as the hallmark of the continued expression of God's reality in the life of the believing community. We see this in two parallel developments. The first is the connection that Yeshua makes between the forgiveness of sins and the love of the Father. Time and time again Yeshua opens our eyes to the real message of God's fatherhood by showing us a God who jealously desires the best for His children. This means that God rescued us in spite of the enormous cost to Himself. It means that Yeshua proclaims God's unquenchable desire to repair the damage that we have created. It finally means that God acts on our behalf as a loving parent for a rebellious child.

The second development is conveyed in the requirement of the believing community to pass on the message of forgiveness. Just as God did not ask us to appeal to His mercy *before* He acted on our behalf, He now expects that this unmerited forgiveness will be reflected in the actions that we take toward those children of the Father, who are alienated from His direct fellowship. Yeshua's instructional prayer of Matthew 6 makes it abundantly clear that the expectation of the believing community is to forgive without conditions, just as we have been forgiven without conditions. Unconditional love demands unconditional forgiveness. There is no requirement on behalf of the offending party to seek repentance, restitution or amends *before* the volitional act of forgiveness occurs. God did not expect such from us. In fact, God knew that the Beast within us made it impossible for us to repent and restore righteousness before unconditional love was given to us. For us, the forgiven of God, there is only one remedy to life's injuries – to forgive others.

The theology of the Lord's Prayer shows that we, who recognize our indebtedness to the Father, have received the unmerited gift of forgiveness. It is this fact of the new order life that propels us to forgive *in like measure* those whom God is wooing into His kingdom. When we understand the change of perspective that accompanies being loved as we are, we find that the manifestations of bestial pride are logically impossible in the kingdom of grace. But when we take to heart the personal transformation that this change of perspective demands of those blessed by grace, we find that the manifestations of pride are not only unthinkable, they are unlivable.

God recognizes that peeling away the layers of bestial behavior is not a swift nor painless process. It occurs in incremental steps. Fortunately, God is infinitely patient with His faltering children. The character of grace is to be found in the expression of the forgiven. It is so simple. Perhaps that is why we find it so difficult. Asking that God's will be done on earth as it is in heaven is asking that we allow God's will to be done in us! Since God does not believe in coercion, our requests for the accomplishment of His will depend on our voluntary abdication of self-in-control. The yardstick for determining just how much we have decided to surrender our fantasy throne can be seen in our progression toward dependence on community.

We must acknowledge that we cannot make ourselves right. We have to feel and know from the very core of who we are that we cannot earn God's blessing. We do not deserve His favor. So from the very start, before we even get out of the blocks, we must face the issue of pride, for pride will never admit to need, will never acknowledge incapacity, will never concede failure. Insofar as we continue *at any level in our lives* to hold on to self-performance, self-status and self-justification, we are subservient to the power of pride. Nothing can go forward until this first issue is settled: who is in control?

What happens when we finally say "Thy will be done" and mean it? We are immediately struck by our own hideousness. We know our powerlessness. We experience our utter helplessness. And we are driven to repentance. Why? Because we have faced the fact that we have been denying the authority and care of our Maker. We have been living the lie of self-sufficiency in the face of God's self-sacrifice. "Forgive us our debts" says something much more profound than the flimsy admission of social indiscretions. It says that we are debtors to God. It says that we recognize and acknowledge that **all of what we are** is God's gift. He is the Maker, we are the made. We are debtors who owe **EVERYTHING**. We are living in perpetual bankruptcy.

And yet God forgives. This forgiveness is not an arm-around-the-shoulder "Forget it. It's OK" exercise. This is forgiveness for what we have systematically destroyed during our entire lives, namely, the wonderful, awesome creation of human beings in the image of God, destined to enjoy a relationship with the Creator forever.

Fields of Blood

We all have the Judas syndrome. It is nothing more, or less, than man without God – without God by our own choosing. Because we want it that way. The Judas in us oozes out in envy, hate, jealousy, anger, revenge, rationalization, denial, greed, arrogance, slander, malice and strife. Because we want it like that. Because we are not going to give in to anyone or anything. Because we want to be important.

The Judas syndrome in us crucifies the Messiah over and over, every time we submit to its delicious temptations. It is as old as humanity. It comes from the drama in the first Garden. It is the desire to run the show. To know more, be more, have more, do more. To be like God.

The Judas syndrome is the exact opposite of the confession of a debtor. And it will lead us to the same place that Judas faced after the betrayal.

There are two fields of blood in every life. One is the result of clutching our own thirty pieces of silver. It is the field that I purchase with what I have taken. It comes from deciding that I can be my own god. The blood in this field is my own, spilled in the death of my fantasy of denial, leaving the shell of what I was made to be. The Beast in me wants only one thing. In the end, the Beast wants me to die in this field.

The other field of blood is one that I am given. It is the one that I received as a gift of adoption. It is filled with the Messiah's blood spilled on my ground so that I can be free. Free of my self-in-control, in order to become myself in His family. I can't receive my gift of adoption as long as I clutch those silver coins. All I need to do is to open my hand and let them go. But that act is impossible for pride to perform.

CHAPTER ELEVEN

Back to the Clearing

But the path of the righteous is like the light of dawn, that shines brighter and brighter until the full day. (Proverbs 4:18)

Fear, guilt, pride. Behind each emotional roadblock, we find the essence of the Beast – self-demanding control. Each manifestation of bestial logic makes us feel isolated from ourselves and others. Each manifestation makes us focus entirely on ourselves, stripping us of healing through others and through outside reality. Each manifestation makes us forget who we are and who God is. In other words, each of these three central roadblocks to recovery are instinctual, bestial behavior, blocking our spiritual awareness while anesthetizing the pain that would heal us.

Now we have discovered another path. We uncovered the God who is faithful, the God who stands by us when fear whispers in our ears. We found the God who is forgiving, the God who shatters the hall-of-shame mirrors. We met the God of love, the God who overcame our self-in-control disease by sacrificing His anointed for His enemies.

In each of these divine encounters, we saw the four keys at work. First, weakness is strength. When we try to bolster our own failing self-courage, when we look within to find that bravery to be, we see only the dark lair of the Beast. Our strength is no strength. We are compromised even in our self-sufficient delusions. The truth is something entirely different. We can be courageous only when we give up trying to be unafraid. We can find help only when we are helpless. We can become human only when we welcome our true powerlessness. Admitting our fear and our shame puts us in position to receive grace. In order to win at this game, we must first admit our weakness, for God is the God of weakness. "Not my will, but thine, be done" is the watchword of graciousness.

Second, openness is protection. Embracing weakness as the essential truth about my life opens the door to God's faithfulness. When fear scratches at the back of my neck, only openness is protection. If I steel myself to God and others and assume the fighter's stance, the Beast within destroys me. But deliberately doing what is unnatural, that is, opening myself to the light of God and others, sharing my hideous secret, letting the Beast be seen, reverses the evil energy and brings me safety. We were never safe alone. Alone we were the constant victims of the Beast. By giving up our need for self-protection, we find safety in the revelation of our secret sins to someone else. Openness leads to forgiveness because the power of secrets is broken. When I stop protecting my hidden shame, God can and does forgive my guilt.

Third, suffering is joy. The pain of guilt, the agony of shame: there is no greater suffering. No physical ailment, no bodily torture can match the unrelenting anguish of the shame of the Beast. And no amount of self-induced medication or self-propelled flight will ever remove it from our souls. If we are to live, we must embrace the pain that heals. We must stop medicating ourselves and welcome that pain. All of our running was just another form of dying. But if we surrender, God makes one absolutely critical promise about the pain that heals. We will not die! To face the Beast, to admit our failure of self-determination, to open ourselves to God and others brings the great pain of healing. And the joy of a life that is clean on the inside. The pain that heals scorches away our disease with the agony of light. But life is in the light. We will not die!

If we will not die from the pain that heals, how can the fourth key be the fact that dying brings life? What does God's promise in the healing pain mean if the fourth key is to die? We already know the answer. Was living with the Beast life? Was fighting the Beast life? Was the fearful union with the Beast life? Was the shame of the Beast life? The Beast never brought us life – not in the manipulation of others, not in the collection of things, not in the myth of control or the delusion of plans. The Beast brought death, a slow strangulation of all that was holy within us. The Beast choked us off from the ones we loved by making loving ourselves impossible. On the field of blood, we discovered the Beast wants one and only one conclusion – that we sacrifice ourselves in the name of self, becoming a carcass disguised as human, the true residence of the father of lies.[19]

Dying is life. But it is not the execution of the person we are intended to be. The death that we need is the death of the Beast – our self-in-control.

---

[19]John 8:44

205

As long as we have intercourse with the Beast, we will be zombies – the living dead. Union with the Beast is death! For us to live, the Beast must die. For the Beast to die, the bastard self that we have made in our frenzied preoccupation with the Beast must die. Until we realize that this is not who we are, we will continue to let the Beast nurture our bastard self. All of our lives the Beast has trained us to think that we cannot be without him. Every day we have listened to his cunning mythology. The voice of the dead has become our guide. We were seduced. Something alien was birthed in us. God calls us back to our true identity. We are not prodigy of the Beast. We are children of the light. It is certain that we will die in this fourth step. But the "we" who will die is the self we have made, not the self that God created. What we built must be destroyed so that what God created can emerge. We are dead anyway. What have we got to lose?

We must return to that clearing inside, the inner vista of emptiness. We do not overcome these roadblocks by attempting to *manage* the four keys. The logic that says we can now maneuver ourselves forward is still bestial logic. We do not *use* the four keys at all. They use us to bring about something that God has in mind. Our only role is to open our eyes to the light. That is the role of ruthless honesty and committed willingness. In the inner clearing, there is only emptiness. There is no room for anything except emptiness. That inner light will reveal everything that our union with the Beast has produced, not all at once, but slowly, inevitably. For the light cannot exist where we hold on to darkness.[20] But the light will flood every hidden crevice that we surrender. That is the nature of light – to expose and to heal.

In the end, we can never find God. Faith is not about finding God. In the end, God will find us! God's light is the light of true reality. It permeates all existence. We are the ones who have hidden from the light. God's light has searched for us in our darkness since we were brought into being. It sears our secret sins, the bricks of our inner prison, in order to find the self we were intended to be. We have only to let it in and the whole world will change. We have only to give up trying to be our own creations.

The Incarnate Man

In Christian theology, the Incarnation is the doctrine about God becoming Man. In the ancient world, this is not a new idea. There are several pagan myths about the gods becoming men. Of course, there are also legends and myths about men becoming gods. In fact, more than one of the emperors of Rome were "elected" to the status of a god by the Senate. The surprising idea expressed in the Bible is neither God becoming a man or a man becoming God. It is that Man is *originally* made in the image of God, and for the Hebrews, this meant that God's active energy was embedded in what it means to be human from the very beginning. Rather than speaking of the incarnation of God, the Bible really talks about the incarnation of Man. To be human is to become like God, that is, to act in

---

[20]John 1:5, 6, 11

207

the ways that God acts, to feel as God feels and to think as God thinks. In Hebrew thought, we might say that God is a *verb* and insofar as we express His activity, we reflect who He is and who we were intended to be.

In this regard, Yeshua demonstrates for us *as a man* what it means to be fully human. He points to himself when asked to reveal the Father. Why? Because he is the *incarnate Man*, being human as it was intended to be a pure reflection of the divine nature. Everything that we have learned from our union with the Beast is built on the mythology of becoming gods, of controlling our world and our fate to meet our desires. But this obscures the true origin and the real purpose. We don't have to become gods. We are already made in such a way that we can exhibit the godly constitution of our origin. The Beast does not wish to become *like God*. That is, in fact, what God intended. The Beast wishes to *be a god*, to have the world as its own.

What we have discovered is that this alien force that wishes to be *a god* can continue only by acquisition. It must gather to itself the world it wishes to control. But the way of salvation is the way of emptiness. <u>What we find when Yeshua discloses God to us is that God is a God of weakness, of openness, of suffering and of death</u>. God is the God of emptiness for emptying oneself on behalf of another is the true character of love. Each of our four keys is a part of the act of love. Each is a step of voluntary self-giving. Incarnate Man is the man emptied of self-in-control in order to voluntarily love the God who has redeemed him. The two go hand in hand. God gives so that we can give up the bestial self. God loves so that we can love the self that God sees us to be.

According to Scripture, Yeshua took on the form of a *doulos*, a slave. In doing so, he learned obedience to the Father. He was the walking, talking, living, breathing example of God's intended purpose for human inner emptiness. He was human as God intended all men to be – the embodiment of Spirit – an empty vessel for God's purposes. Yeshua showed us that every moment of our lives is, in reality, a moment of surrender and dependence. He showed us that second-by-second interaction with the Father meant a life of sacrificial love in joyful service to God. He showed us that the vision of the Spirit guides us beyond our search for control, for status, for attraction, for possession. Yeshua showed us that life comes from delight in God's way, fulfilling of God's desires, attuned to God's reality. He walked where we walk in the dark night of fear. He felt what we feel in the temptations to let the Beast seduce our humanity. He was asked, as we are, to succeed through self-sufficiency. He was a man just as we are men and women. But he was more than we are. He surrendered to God.

Surrender

The Incarnate Man is the person of surrender. No one can be weak without capitulation. No one can be open to emptiness without giving up control. No one can see joy in suffering without submission to healing pain. No one can die to self without abandonment to God. The magic of surrender is that there is no magic. There is no secret formula, incantation, mantra or special knowledge needed before surrender can be successful. There is no philosophy to learn, religion to espouse, sect to join or therapy to perform. Surrender has nothing to do with trying. That is why it is so hard. It is so hard because it is backwards from everything that we have ever wanted to hear from the lips of the Beast. We have wanted to earn our way, to demand our rights, to be able to negotiate our freedom. But it will never be. Surrender is so hard because it is human and we are not.[21]

---

[21] A recent retreat of people in recovery produced the following behaviors associated with the experience of surrender: 1. Admitting that I am an addict, 2. Substituting good relationships for bad ones, 3. Sharing my story and my feelings, 4. Praying, 5. Going to meetings, 6. Trusting people in other areas of my life, 7. Reaching out for help, 8. Permitting myself to have "not-in-control" experiences and not running from the feelings, 9. Letting my feelings out, 10. Putting aside my need to know, 11. Giving up the idea that my past determines my future, 12. Celebrating a healing experience, 13. Confessing promptly when I falter, 14. Choosing the right path, 15. Being obedient right now, 16. Doing what is the best thing for me, 17. Accepting the pain of my emotions, 18. Giving up the right to medicate myself, 19. Forgiving myself, 20. Giving up a trigger to an old pattern - breaking an old habit, 21. Accepting the value that others give me, 22. Getting rid of the "if you only knew" thinking, 23. Accepting the value that God gives me, 24. Acting "as if" I could be all that I want to be, 25. Doing my daily diligence, 26. Congratulating myself for a successful 24 hour period of sobriety, 27. Accepting God's gifts to me, 28. Being willing to see myself as a truly am and owning it, 29. Making healthy decisions, 30. Giving myself permission to get well, 31. Willing myself to be visible to others, 32. Giving up an excuse that I used, 33. Doing something against my natural inclination (against my addict wishes).

The Beast has been alive in us for as long as we can remember. We are no longer the wonderfully innocent human infants that we once were. We no longer know the truth of utter dependence as an ever-present fact of our being. We are aliens in human skin.

ALIEN

The alien
Infects me.
My mind bent toward his purposes.
My heart filled with his desires.
My will corrupted by his lusts.

I invited him in
On promises of freedom,
On hopes of success,
On dreams of grandeur.

And he resides in my house
At my request,
Slowing torturing me with exquisite pain,
Closing my doors and windows,
Opening the inner stairwells
To lower and lower floors
Away from the light.

I am being changed into
The alien.

The mystery of surrender is the mystery of emptiness. It is a process of osmosis rather than a planned progression. We experience surrender only when we choose to stand in the light. From the edge of the clearing, we will continue to be ravaged by the Beast. From the shadow world of our present lives, we look out across the beautiful light of the expanse. The Beast within clamors for retreat. He convulses, screams, cajoles, begs. Anything to prevent us from doing what only true humans can do. The Beast within can never surrender to the light. Light is death for the Beast – and life for true humanity. At the edge of that great emptiness we feel all of the fear that the Beast can manufacture. We are racked with the tentacles of past shame and present guilt. The Beast literally batters us with overwhelming prideful resistance.

We cannot surrender by observing the light in the clearing. Experiencing surrender is not achieved by thinking about it, reading about it, analyzing it. Not even now as we analyze this event. No one can ever surrender from the shadows. We cannot feel the light on us until we step out of the shade. Then we will know surrender because it will surround us. To experience surrender we must do surrendering. Grace can't find us in the dark.

The light seeks. The light burns. The light soothes. The light calls. To be human once again. To step into the light and let emptiness take me. To give up all of my trying to be what I could never become in order to be what I have always wanted. To be free in the light.

The night is almost gone, and the day is at hand. Let us therefore lay aside the deeds of darkness and put on the armor of light. (Romans 13:12)

Use this simple prayer to affirm your desire to step into the light. It is my prayer too. You can supply the words for the blanks. Just ask the Beast what he wants you to keep for himself. But remember, speaking this prayer from the shadows is not surrender. Surrender is stepping into emptiness, *without words*.

God, my Father,

Give me the strength this day to surrender my feelings to you. I am helpless to resist the power of my addiction to _____ without you. When each opportunity comes where I might run to my Beast in order to ease my pain, make me aware of my real feelings and help me surrender them to you. I know that you love me even in my struggles with _____. I know that you are able and willing to rescue me from my addictive prison. I know that you care for me even when I feel like I am all alone. I give myself to you to be used as you will today. Not my will but thine be done.
Amen

HOME

Paused at night
Saw the light
Needed "Stop"
Wanted "Drop"
Spent my day
Far away
Spent my year
Far from here
Spent my life
Torn in strife
Not at home
Out alone
All the faces
All the places
Empty miles
Shallow smiles

Bring me back now
I'm tired of dying.

CHAPTER TWELVE

Body Consciousness II

We are back at the beginning. This is also the mystery of surrender. We often return to the beginning when we step into the light. There is so much ground to recover when we finally see where we are going. And God is so patient in guiding us over that so-familiar path. But now the beginning is the beginning of humanness. When we started this journey toward the light, we were aware only of our bestial illness. We had acid indigestion of the soul. Bestial illness, with all of its discomfort, left us without direction because it ultimately left us alone. We discovered that God's light of grace was pushing into our prison walls all along. We realized that we were not victims in that prison cell. We were active participants with the Beast, holding up the very walls that kept the light out. Our fear, shame and pride fueled the efforts to keep God out, but those efforts only kept death in.

Now that we begin surrendering our denial of humanness to the only One who knew who we really were in the first place, we find that we are part of a new body, a new community. Now we belong to the body of the forgiven. Surrender-ers like us. Molting their bestial skins in the light of God's love, they share our emptiness. They hold our hands. Some have been moving toward the light longer than we have. Some are just starting to feel the healing pain. But they are part of us. We find unity in sharing secrets. We find fellowship in opening wounds. We find forgiveness in suffering together. We learn to die together. We are no longer alone.

Ahead of us is our one true guide. He walked the trail before us. He felt every stone, found every crevice, faced every enemy. He knows this pathway toward the light better than we ever will. And he knows us. He gives us his hand as he speaks two promises:

I will never desert you, nor will I ever forsake you.[22]

And lo, I am with you always, even to the end of the age.[23]

In the process of surrender, we are constantly reminded that God guides us toward more and more light. This means that we will become aware of the extent of our inner darkness as never before. What we thought was only a small rift between the person God wants us to be, and the self we have become, will slowly be disclosed as a great chasm. God always focuses His attention on the remaining darkness of our bestial selves. We will know the serenity of surrender in this continuous unveiling as long as we are willing to remain in the light. The road will get easier, but not now.

That first step into the light of the clearing will probably be accompanied by a compulsive torment greater than we have ever known. The reason is quite simple. For years, the Beast allowed us to

---

[22]Hebrews 13:5
[23]Matthew 28:20

subordinate our values to our feelings. We were driven, not by what we held to be true and lovely, but by what we felt in our agony, abandonment and despair. Until we took that first step, we always used the mythology of the Beast to medicate our wounds. Light does not medicate. It cauterizes. This first step will be accompanied by finally feeling the real pains we have buried in the darkness for so many years. The Beast will do everything possible to drive us back to cover. The Beast knows that light heals, and that light kills disease and addiction.

For our sakes, it's wonderful that God is infinitely patient. He knows where we have to go and how we have to get there. His revelation of the depth of our darkness will often cause us to want to return to the "shelter" of the Beast. Each new layer of bestial logic will beg us to retreat to the shadows once again. We will feel fear. We will suffer guilt and shame. We will experience prideful resistance. All of this is to be expected, and to be counted as a *blessing of grace*, for it means that we are becoming human at last. God is finding us in our darkness and leading us home. Our battle with perfectionism will have to be surrendered along with our powerlessness over each dark recess that God gently opens. Now that we know the truth about fear, guilt and shame, we have every reason to celebrate these cycles. They are the results of surrender. In fact, celebrating them is an act of surrender itself for it is an act that leads us in the opposite direction of our natural (bestial) tendency.

There is another promise that we need in our daily meditation in order to combat the wailing of the

Beast. It summarizes our need for new thinking, for new direction. It offers help and hope. It reminds us to let go and let God do the rest.

Trust in the Lord with all your heart, and do not lean on your own understanding. In all your ways acknowledge Him, and He will make your paths straight. (Proverbs 3:5-6)

For us, the key word in this verse is *straight*. The root word means to be level, straight, just or lawful. In its derivations, it is often connected with the idea of law keeping and uprightness. It is both the work of God for man, as in this verse, and also the work of man for God (Isaiah 40:3). It characterizes the person who is blameless, a person of discernment. God grants us the ability to recognize His law and to walk in it. In one important derivative, the word is an attributive adjective of God Himself, emphasizing His righteousness and His reign over all people. The person who is judged to have straight paths has that quality of heart that enables him to be obedient to God's will. This promise claims that our dependence on God will allow Him to straighten out our lives. We need not struggle with the mechanics of how this will be done. We are asked only to trust Him and not ourselves and He will do the rest. It is a blessing for those of us in recovery to know that God is willing and able to repair what we have damaged if we only surrender ourselves to Him in all our endeavors.

How Well Am I?

When we first encountered the test of well-being, we should have titled it, "How Sick Am I?" for we

218

were sick indeed. We were infected with the "sickness unto death." Now our self-exam can become a test of wellness. "How well am I?" I am well indeed! The Beast in me is dying in the light of surrender. My emptiness is growing. I am becoming human.

1. *The people in my life who matter most to me really understand who I am. They love me regardless of anything that I have done. I feel more and more open with them.*

My surrender of the bestial secret lets God speak to me through others. I find that I am not alone. The reason that others can accept me as I am is that they also struggle with the Beast. They need to share their secret as much as I do. And when we all begin to share those dark places, God meets us in the light of our common humanity.

2. *I feel truly free.*

I could never be free as long as I pursued "imagined" freedom. To be truly free, I have to become a slave to the light. My real freedom is the decision to be bound to surrender to God and His graciousness for me. I am free when I bind myself to His instruction for living. License brought me nothing but the Beast. Obligation brings me peace.

3. *I have completely forgiven all those who have intentionally or unintentionally injured or disappointed me over the years.*

How could I forgive others when I could not forgive myself? Even now I am just beginning to realize how long I have held on to my unforgiveness of others. The task of forgiving is forever, but each time I do forgive, I feel the light pour into my soul. Forgiving another becomes the balm that heals my own wounds. I continue forgiving.

4. *My conscience is clear and I have a positive sense of well-being about those actions that I deliberately or accidentally took in the past that harmed or mistreated myself or others. I have completely forgiven myself.*

Being able to forgive others does more than release the burden of anger that I have carried. It also opens the door to see myself for what I am—one of the same ones who needs forgiveness from me. God has declared that He forgives me. I have surrendered my desire to hold on to my wounds. My past no longer determines my future. My past is not erased, but I have left the repair work to God. I am ready to become human.

5. *I awake each day with a renewed sense of purpose and celebration for the life that I lead.*

I surrender my day to God. I have discovered that I can do nothing else if I want to live as a human being. I celebrate the light I have been given and the darkness that has been revealed. I celebrate my birth day, this day, for what it is – an experience of wonder at finally being me.

6. *I know that I am cared for, that my very existence is part of a greater, living pattern.*

Surrender brings with it the blessing that God cares for me. I am no longer responsible for my ultimate destiny. He has something in mind, something wonderful because it is about me, His child. I am responsible for just this: today! Today is the day that I choose to be human, to be like my Father, to be His child in His world.

7. *I know what it means to love and be loved, and I am presently immersed in this deep understanding. Life is joyful for me.*

Slowly, patiently, God is teaching me love. Love is also part of emptiness. When I sought to fill myself with what I thought was love, I inherited only self-adoration. I may never know this secret of emptiness, but I have some clues. In the clearing, the light of my life is being transformed into the love of God. Thank you, Lord. I waited so long in the dark that I almost forgot what I really wanted.

8. *I welcome the responsibilities I have chosen for my life knowing that they serve a higher purpose, no matter how trivial they may seem at the moment. I am content.*

Surrender lets me live outside of myself. I am learning to rejoice in the circumstances of just being alive. God leads, I follow. Nothing more needs to be done for me to know who I am. Now my way is the way of a peace that passes understanding. Contentment. I sought it all my life only to find that it could never be a possession. I had to give myself away to a purpose greater than myself in order to experience being content.

9. *My struggles with fear, anxiety, guilt, pride, anger and despair are passing emotions that I am able to surrender to the greater purpose that I enjoy today.*

J. R. R. Tolkien said it in *The Hobbit*. "The road goes ever on." As God reveals my darkness, I am asked only to surrender. Nothing more is needed for God to heal my wounds and repair the damage. Nothing less is required for me to live as a human being. My road goes ever on.

10. *I am not afraid to die.*

Light begets light. The death that I feared has already happened. I died when I stepped into the light. There is no death in the light. Why should I fear what cannot be taken from me? There is only life beyond the grave of self.

An Addict's Prayer

One thing is certain. Wherever the Beast has stripped our lives of joy, comfort and peace, he has removed our humanness and left us addicts. Surrender begins by admitting to ourselves that we cannot control the Beast, that we are his captives, and that only God can save us. This is the glorious victory of being a *conscious* addict. Until I knew my own degradation, I did not *need* God. Religion may have been a fixture in my life, but I lived (I thought) without conscious unconditional dependence on the Father. Now I know better. My curse has saved me from myself. I invite you to get on your knees with me. The words will come.

Our Father in heaven, we thank You that we are addicts. We thank You that You have let us see how enslaved we were to the Beast within. Now we know that we cannot live without You. Now we know that our very existence must be placed in Your hands every moment of our days. Take us as we are and do with us as You please. We have no life but Yours. We never did. Not our will, but Yours, be done.

In the end, life must be either a curse or an Amen.

Amen, Lord, Amen.

"Man cannot be good unless he strives to be holy."
Abraham Heschel

POSTSCRIPT

Usually postscripts are afterthoughts, things added to complete ideas that were a bit fragmented in the body of the work. This postscript is not of that kind. This postscript is *crucial* to the end game.

This book is an *analysis* of what it means to confront the Beast within. It is an instructional guide for dealing with the Beast, or better, for allowing the emptiness of humanity in the expanse of God to find us and rescue us from the clutches of the Beast. Make no mistake here. *You cannot get yourself out* of the mess you have created. The more you try, the more you empower the Beast to hold you back. Time and time again you will come to the very precipice of surrender only to see yourself pulling back one step into the shadows that are so comforting – and humiliating.

The problem is not *thinking about the solution*. The problem is *engaging the solution*. We all *know* that we are in trouble, that our efforts in the past have failed, that we are essentially powerless to stop this decline into non-human existence. We *know* it, but we are unable to change. Why? Because *knowing* isn't enough. The Beast loves knowledge because knowledge alone is powerless for change. Yes, we were taught that knowledge is power, but this is a manifest lie when it comes to the Beast. Knowledge is powerless to defeat the Beast because it is already co-opted by the Beast. In Hebrew, knowing does not exist without doing. If I assert that I *know* something, but my life does not reflect the change in behavior implied by what I know, then in Hebrew *I did not know it*! Arnold Bennett tells us why this is the case.

"There can be no knowledge without emotion. We may be aware of a truth, yet until we have felt its force, it is not ours. To the cognition of the brain must be added the experience of the soul."

Thus, this postscript. You cannot recover until you *feel recovery*! How can that happen?

Not quickly!

That's the rub. The Beast acts immediately. Anesthetizing our shame, guilt and fear is virtually instantaneous. As soon as I initiate the addictive cycle, I feel better, at least temporarily. Recovery doesn't work this way. It is a long, slow process. It hurts. It causes anxiety. It confuses our emotional state of mind. We want the fix, but recovery says we must forego the immediate for the sake of long-term sanity. And that means we will have to deal with the emotional trauma of *unsatisfied* need. Of course, it really isn't unsatisfied *need*, is it? It is really *desire*. We could live *without* the addictive fix, but life would immediately be harder, now. Recovery means hurting now to celebrate later, and hurting now is about *emotional* disturbance. This is why I can *know* what I should do and find myself not doing it. The emotional need is stronger than the rational choice.

If we are going to play this game with the Beast, we will have to be prepared to deal with our emotional dysfunctions. We will have to talk to ourselves over and over, reminding ourselves that, yes, right now it hurts, but it is supposed to hurt because it is healing. Right now, we need to *feel* what it *might be like* to not go through this the next time, and then make this time the next time.

There is one more crucial bit to this postscript. If we successfully manage to confront the emotional trauma of this moment and not engage the immediate numbing of the addiction, the Beast is more than likely to use this as ammunition against us. "You see," he says, "you *can* overcome. You just did it. Don't you feel better? You successfully resisted. You're on the right track. Now you *know* you can recover. So, why not reward yourself for your victory?"

Ah, he is so clever.

Here's a hint. Stay with the pain. It is real. The rest is seduction. Eventually the pain will turn into *real* healing. Eventually – or maybe sooner.

May God be with you.

ABOUT THE AUTHOR

Skip Moen, D. Phil. (Oxford) is the author of

Spiritual Restoration, Vols. 1-3

Guardian Angel

The Lucky Life

Cross Word Puzzles

God, Time and the Limits of Omniscience

Jesus Said to Her

31: Days of Transformation

Crossing: The Struggle for Self-Identity

He has written thousands of word studies of the biblical vocabulary.

All of his work can be found at
skipmoen.com

Made in the USA
Columbia, SC
27 June 2018